Calculated Risk

The Modern

Entrepreneur's

Handbook

Michael J Palumbo

Library of Congress Cataloging-in-Publication Data:
ISBN 978-0-9974595-0-0 EAN-13 9 780997 459500
Printed in the United States of America, New York, New York
First Edition April, 2016. First Printing April 15, 2016.

Calculated Risk: The Modern Entrepreneur's Handbook

Dedication

To my mother, JoAnne, who taught me to never stop seeking knowledge, and to my father, Marino, who taught me to not sweat the small stuff.

Acknowledgements

I wish to thank Mark Whistler, Andrew Koroneos, and Taylor Steffens for their contributions and support throughout the process of writing this book.

Table of Contents

Calculated Risk: The Modern Entrepreneur's Handbook

Prologue

Calculated Risk: The Modern Entrepreneur's Handbook is intended to help founders and executives navigate today's business world from the first moments of idea conception, all the way through an exit.

In essence, Calculated Risk: The Modern Entrepreneur's Handbook is a guidebook for founders and executives seeking an insider's perspective on achieving startup success - written by someone who started a prop trading group in Chicago that turned into a highly successful US stock options business, a firm that was one of the largest equity options trading groups in the country in the late 1990's and the early 2000's.

Throughout the entire experience there were many highs and lows, but in the end, we created a significant amount of wealth, *well in excess of $100 million dollars*.

The story includes starting my own firm from scratch and then once it was successful, becoming the angel investor in the fintech firm GETCO, which I ended up exiting to a private equity group at a valuation over $1.7 billion.

Within this publication entrepreneurs will find information they will not learn in business school.

While there might be other methods of starting your own business, Calculated Risk: The Modern Entrepreneur's Handbook is what I found along the way - *that actually worked.*

I believe the performance of my company, Third Millennium Trading, and GETCO speak for the value of the model I have created.

Calculated Risk: The Modern Entrepreneur's Handbook was developed through many mistakes, but more importantly, *by learning as a result of doing.*

So let the twenty years of experience I have gained, including some good decisions as well as mistakes, help to guide you in your own entrepreneurial pursuits.

~ Michael J Palumbo

1 Getting the Idea

Coming up with an idea for a great technology company, product, service, or business overall is obviously one of the most important parts of Calculated Risk: The Modern Entrepreneur's Handbook.

After all, without a great idea so many businesses are doomed to fail. And unfortunately, the bottom line is: _all ideas are not equal_, and no matter how talented the company founders are; you cannot sell ice to Eskimos.

A great idea is paramount to the success of an enterprise.

When a great business idea is unearthed, a wildfire of growth and success can, and often does, ensue.

With the aforementioned in mind, over the next few pages we are going to discuss a few logical "stress tests" I have developed to qualify your company's idea, technology, product, or service.

Then, in Chapter 2 we will discuss Identifying the Markets for the idea.

Observation of Need | Relevancy Test

The most important part of coming up with a great idea is observation, basically people watching. Many of those who come up with the best business ideas are simply the best observers of people and what goes on in society. They are really "super observers" who have an innate ability to figure out what other people need, often before these people even truly realize they need it themselves.

Take Uber for example. The larger business of taxicabs had been around for so long, it was hard to imagine there was much possibility of improvement, especially since it is such a highly regulated industry. Then Uber came along, and as those who have used the service know, it compares very favorably to taking a regular cab. Uber identified a need that was likely in the back of many consumers' minds: a relatively clean, inexpensive, reliable, prompt alternative to greasy old cabs, with the fare and tipping completely simplified.

There was no more waiting on a curb waving a hand in the air. Uber created an app that allows people to easily and conveniently summon a ride from their smartphone. Now that Uber is around, the need people were not even truly cognizant of has been fulfilled, and Uber's growth has superbly matched the "quality of the need." Funny thing though, before Uber and Lyft showed up on the scene, most people who now love the services probably did not even know directly that they needed or wanted it.

UBER RAPIDLY STOLE MARKET SHARE FROM CABS

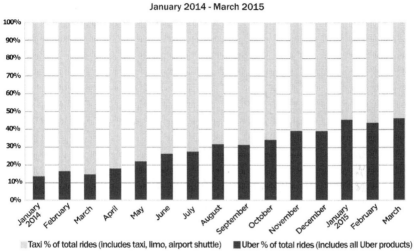

UBER ON THE RISE NATIONWIDE
January 2014 - March 2015

Taxi % of total rides (includes taxi, limo, airport shuttle)   Uber % of total rides (includes all Uber products)

Source: Sharing the Road: Business Travelers Increasingly Choose Uber, Certify.com

They likely wished for something better, but had not quite put their finger on how their itch could be scratched. Uber invented a service (utilizing technology) for people before they were even truly aware, or at least fully appreciated that they wanted and/or needed it.

Steve Jobs said, "A lot of times, people don't know what they want until you show it to them."

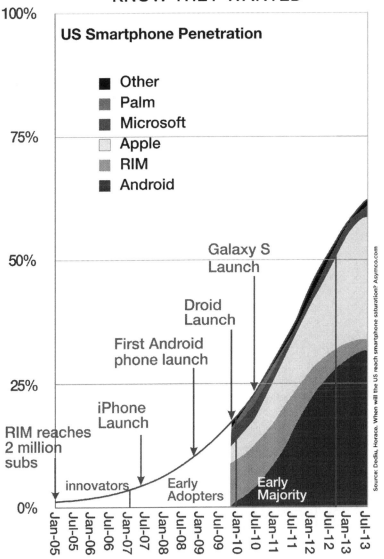

iPHONE GAVE MOST AMERICANS A PRODUCT THEY DID NOT KNOW THEY WANTED

US Smartphone Penetration

- ■ Other
- ■ Palm
- ■ Microsoft
- □ Apple
- ■ RIM
- ■ Android

Many consumers never knew they needed an iPhone or any other smartphone before the product actually existed. And while Steve Jobs and Apple were not the ones who invented smartphones, they did take an existing product idea and made it so appealing to consumers that Apple's position in the cell phone market grew like wildfire.

What I am talking about is understanding what people need and then figuring out what type of technology and business can make it happen.

The best entrepreneurs are the ones who are the best at observing people and society, and are able to figure out what consumers or businesses need, before they know what they need.

One of my first great business successes was with my company, Third Millennium Trading, at the Chicago Board Options Exchange, which I started in 1996. Back then computers had just begun to be used in a meaningful way in trading. What I identified was the need for quicker trade execution and deeper (more liquid) options markets.

Basically what I figured out was that there was a strong need for a "one-stop options shop" for the entire US Stock Market. There were other companies doing this, but getting an actual trade done was sometimes a slow process, especially when there was a lack of liquidity.

I identified the need to shorten the amount of time it took to get a trade done, while also providing more liquidity than other firms across the entire US equity options market.

Trading was not actually done on computers at this time, at least not like today. I figured out a way to evaluate risk very quickly, which allowed my firm to respond to trade requests in seconds, while other firms were taking minutes. This may not sound like a big difference, but in trading every second is crucial. Today, trading is done in milliseconds, and the game has changed. But in the late 1990's and early 2000's my innovation within US options trading allowed my company to become one of the largest US options and equities trading firms in America (if not the world) in a very short period of time.

I was also able to create over $100 million dollars in wealth by innovating the concepts of speed and depth within options markets. But it all began by first identifying a need, and then figuring out a way to fulfill that need.

In 2000, I hedged my company by being the original venture capital investor in the high frequency trading firm GETCO. Trading execution via computers was quickly becoming *the new standard* at the turn of the century. GETCO had identified the need for even more speed - electronically. In essence, I hedged my own company, betting on a company that developed a technology that would increase speed and liquidity even more.

The bet paid off as GETCO became a massive success. By the time GETCO was sold to private equity, the little company I had backed with just $750,000 at a valuation under $5 million grew to over $1.7 billion in a period of eight years.

With both my own company and my investment in GETCO, the bottom line was that a need was identified, and a business/technology was created to fulfill the need. Success ensued in both cases.

Of importance, I would like to note that because my company, Third Millennium Trading, did not have the technology to keep up with the way trading was moving towards even faster computerized executions at the turn of the new century, I hedged my company through my investment in GETCO.

One important characteristic of the modern business climate is that technology is constantly changing and evolving. While this might seem like a *"no-brainer, duh!"* kind of statement, we need to examine it in more detail.

The famous hockey player Wayne Gretzky once said, "I skate to where the puck is going, not where it has been."

What this means in relation to a great idea is simply that any great idea is great - only so long as it is relevant in terms of technology and the market.

Basically, the best ideas in the world are the ideas that skate to where the puck is going to be, not where it is at right now, or has been. Great ideas innovate and shake up an industry or create a whole new industry, and are *ahead* of their time.

A truly great business idea takes into account where the current marketplace is heading and anticipates coming technological innovations.

Moreover, great ideas usually give the world something it did not even know it needed. The world maybe had an itchy feeling there was something that could be better, but the new idea had not come into existence just yet. Once this new idea is deployed though, the world cannot live without it.

But all ideas are only relevant as long as they are on the leading edge of their industry or market. In the case of my company, Third Millennium Trading, even when we were in full swing, I still recognized technology was constantly evolving and changing within the options and trading industry. I essentially skated to where the puck was going to be *next* by investing in the high frequency trading startup, GETCO.

VOLUME GROWTH IN THE TRADING INDUSTRY DURING THE LATE 1990'S AND EARLY 2000'S

Options Clearing Corporation - Number of Trades per year 1973-2014

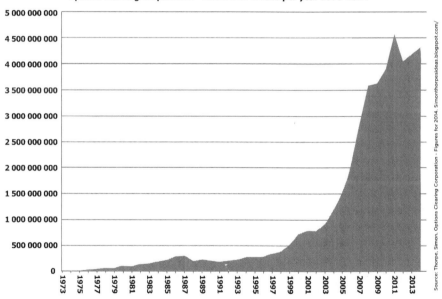

Source: Thorpe, Simon, Options Clearing Corporation - Figures for 2014, Simonthorpesideas.blogspot.com/

Great ideas must come to you with significant understanding of how technology can help bring about this concept, but even more so, why the idea is relevant to where the market or technology is going to be.

In addition, it is so very important to look at technology *not where it is now*, but *where it is going to be five years from now*, when your company is actually up and rolling.

The question is: *will your idea still be relevant?*

The Geography Test

Next up in evaluating any business idea is what I call the Geography Test. Basically, when entrepreneurs come up with a great idea they often fail to ask themselves how relevant the idea is on a mass scale. Going back to the Uber example, the idea works because it is relevant across the board. The taxi industry - until Uber showed up - was basically the same everywhere. Uber's idea provided a needed service to people not only in San Francisco, but in just about every city in the world. In other words, the idea was not only timely and relevant, but also hugely needed and scalable. Why? Because it would fulfill an unrecognized need everywhere. Uber's concept passed the Geography Test.

Airbnb is another great example. The company developed a website allowing for anyone to rent out their home, apartment, space, or even just spare bedrooms to travelers worldwide.

Airbnb completely shook up the hotel and travel market globally, empowering regular people to earn money renting out their extra space on a short-term basis.

THE LARGE NUMBER OF LISTINGS IN NON-U.S. CITIES SHOWS THE GLOBAL RELEVANCE OF AIRbnb

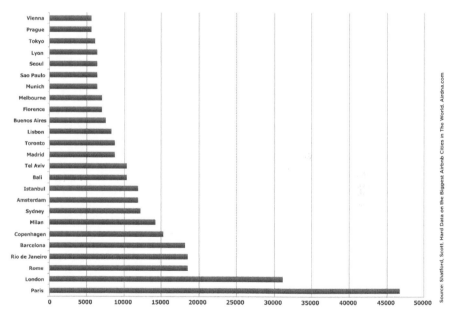

The idea behind Airbnb was relevant everywhere. Not only that, the idea also created a platform which enabled others to make money too, much like Uber. Moreover, as I already mentioned, the idea was relevant in terms of technology, while also shaking up an old industry (hotel and travel) in a new and innovative way.

By the way, Airbnb was founded in 2008, but by April of 2014 the company had over 300,000 listings in 33,000 cities in 192 countries and had a valuation of over $10 billion.[1]

Airbnb as well as Uber, as ideas/business concepts definitely passed the Geography Test; both companies had great ideas that identified a need people wanted before they even knew they wanted it. Henceforth, Uber and Airbnb have grown like wildfire. More about the wildfire concept coming in Chapter 2, Identifying the Markets, but for now, please just understand that Uber's, Airbnb's, and Apple's ideas - in and of themselves – were not just chasing something already in existence, but skated to where the puck would be next, utilizing technology to do so.

Both Uber and Airbnb are leaders in their space because they passed the Geography Test, and then built a competitive advantage over other players to

---

[1] Airbnb.com, Wikipedia page. Accessed: March, 2015. http://en.wikipedia.org/wiki/Airbnb

maintain their position. This competitive advantage can be called a *moat*, because it protects the company from its adversaries. In both companies' cases, their moats consisted of developing a recognizable brand, which was developed due to their respective first mover advantages. Both companies were the first large player in their spaces, and because they were both easy to use and reliable, word spread, and this gave them a leg up on their competition. Both companies have been able to maintain this leadership position by being viewed as the industry leader, even though good alternatives have come along after.

If you keep your customers happy, they will return, and if you have a first mover advantage and execute well, it should result in a leadership position. This is definitely true in the case of Uber and Airbnb. We will talk much more about building a moat later in Chapter 5: Entrepreneurialism in the Modern Age.

The Feasibility Test

Now let us talk about what I call the Feasibility Test.

In a nutshell, it is not enough to just have a great idea; rather, you must be able to execute on the idea as well. It is truly the "acid test" where the rubber hits the road.

Often, entrepreneurs believe they have the best idea around, and they commence business only to struggle endlessly, until they finally end up out of business.

If the idea was so great, then why did the business flounder and eventually fail? Perhaps it was not the idea that was flawed.

Inability to execute is a cold, harsh reality in many entrepreneurial situations. When the idea is great, but revenue, or some other type of growth-related metric, is not there, something under the hood is likely broken. Unfortunately all too often it is not the idea, it is management.

Here is what is really important to glean from the Feasibility Test; investors and venture capital guys like me are not looking solely for profitability. Sometimes, we are hardly looking for any profitability at all, especially in startups seeking seed funding. What we are looking for are metrics that show some type of *traction*.

Traction is the key word here. Increasing revenue, rising subscriber-base, organic user-growth; these are all things that offset profitability. Why? Because what many entrepreneurs do not understand is profitability can be dialed in at a later date. The first and most important hurdle to tackle is: Can the idea get traction?

If the business cannot show some type of traction, either the idea or management is flawed.

Facebook is a great example. In the beginning they were not making much money, but their initial investor saw huge opportunity through user growth. Peter Theil, the founder of PayPal, invested $500,000 in Facebook in 2004, in the form of a convertible note.

Part of the deal was the loan would be converted into equity if Facebook attained 1.5 million users by the end of 2004.[2] Even though the revenue was not there, Theil saw traction through user growth. Traction leads to revenue, which should lead to profitability.

Facebook passed the Feasibility Test because not only was it a great idea, but Zuckerberg and his cohorts were proving their ability to execute by achieving rapid user growth.

Another aspect of the Feasibility Test is determining whether adequate technology infrastructure exists, while also questioning whether the world is ready for the concept as well. Remember Steve Jobs' quote from earlier in this chapter, "A lot of times, people don't know what they want until you show it to them."

---

[2] History of Facebook, Wikipedia. First angel investment (Series A). Accessed: April, 2015.
http://en.wikipedia.org/wiki/History_of_Facebook

The thing is, everything is relative, and often people do not know what they want until you show them. However, sometimes the world just is not ready for a new idea too; either that or the technology to make the idea happen has not evolved enough quite yet. Take the retail dotcoms in the 1990's for example.

Selling goods online through websites was a great idea, but the technology was not there before the turn of the new century, and the world was not quite ready for a new retail paradigm yet.

First, communication speeds were nowhere near where they are today. Many people were still using dial-up modems at home which made the online shopping process slow and painful. Second, smartphones and iPads were not in existence, meaning people could not shop on the go, like during the morning commute on the train to work. Third, the online checkout process was not very user friendly. Basically, technology just had not quite evolved to a point where the idea of online shopping could be embraced by the masses. And as a result, many of the online e-tailers failed when the dotcom bubble burst.

EToys.com is a great example. The online retailer commenced business in 1997 to what appeared to be a great reception by consumers and the press. By 1999, the company seemed to be one of the hottest online retailers around.

The company even held an IPO in mid-1999. IPO shares were issued at $20, but by the end of the first day of trading, the stock shot up to $76.[3]

THE IMMEDIATE DROP IN eTOYS.COM STOCK PRICE

However, in 2001 the company filed for bankruptcy. While there were some legal problems along the way, the real reason the company failed is the world simply was not ready for the idea just yet, and the company did not have the war chest to wait it out.

---

[3] eToys.com; Wikipedia. Accessed: April, 2015. http://en.wikipedia.org/wiki/EToys.com

Today, online retailers are booming. Previously though, technology just had not evolved enough, and there were not even smartphones yet.

Clearly, smartphones allow people to shop more easily online today. The large-scale Amazon model for online retail was not fully attainable 15 years ago.

Let us look at the Amazon model to examine why the online retailer was able to survive the dotcom bubble. Amazon was founded in 1994, with an IPO to follow in 1997. The company did not turn a profit until the first quarter of 2001.

So how was Amazon able to survive the dotcom bubble? In my opinion, it came down to expectations, and the ability to wait out an adverse environment until the world was ready for the company's business model. In the company's initial business plan, Bezos stated the company did not expect to see a profit for at least four or five years. In fact, when the company did turn its first profit in 2001, it made a mere $5 million profit on $1 billion in sales.[4]

---

[4] Amazon.com; Wikipedia. Accessed: April, 2015. http://en.wikipedia.org/wiki/Amazon.com

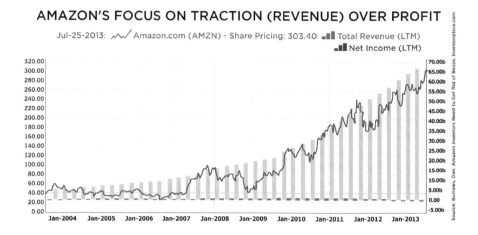

As I mentioned before, while Wall Street was moaning and groaning about Amazon's lethargic profit growth, for savvy investors, other metrics of feasibility were clearly apparent. The metrics I am talking about here are: market share of online sales, gross revenue, and users.

Amazon had staying power in the middle of the dotcom shakeout, but more importantly the executive team knew that profit would eventually be dialed in, as long as other metrics of traction showed growth. And today, the company is the world's largest online retailer.

Not only was Amazon a great idea, but the company continually showed traction when other companies that blew up in the dotcom bubble failed. And the thing to remember is the traction (feasibility)

Amazon showed was seen through metrics apart from profitability. In today's electronic world, it is always great to see early profitability, but talented executive teams and savvy investors understand profitability is not the only metric of success by which to gauge a great idea meeting the road with solid traction.

The Competency Test

Finally, I would like to offer that even after you have an idea that passes the previous tests, you should ask yourself one final question: "Am I the right person to make this happen?"

This is a very important part of the idea equation. And you must answer this with complete honesty. You must do what many people find very difficult and go outside of yourself to evaluate your skills, your passion, and ultimately your level of competency for this task.

The hardest person to criticize and evaluate in life will always be yourself, and those who truly understand themselves and their skill set are some of the wisest people around.

Can you take this idea and make it a reality? What are your skills that uniquely qualify you for this task? And importantly, are you *passionate* about this project?

The greatest business leaders in history, Bill Gates, Henry Ford, Steve Jobs were not only blessed with a perfect skill set to perform as an entrepreneur at the highest level, but they had the *passion* to see their ideas through to fruition.

I bring up some of the greatest entrepreneurs of the 20th and early 21st centuries only because that is the standard you are seeking to achieve. They are the best examples of where competency meets drive and equates to success. Do you have what it takes to take your idea to the finish line? Is your attention to detail good enough to go from zero to a company employing tens, hundreds or even thousands? Because the best ideas in the world will not make it past the first few months without a founder (or group of founders) capable of doing what it takes to beat the odds and create incredible value for themselves and others. And they are long odds! Even with a great idea, the odds are against you to make this happen. Realize this, and objectively evaluate your own ability to take this all the way. And if there is a skill or set of skills you lack, by all means go out and find that in a partner. It does not mean you cannot succeed, but it may mean you need help.

There is no shame in seeking help, and if you do need help, say on the marketing end, or maybe in programming or other areas of tech, you better find it or this whole project will fail.

A great example of a failure of the Competency Test comes from an unlikely source.

Sony has been an innovative company at the forefront of technological development for decades, but it showed a clear lack of the attention to detail I mentioned earlier in this section when it developed Betamax.

As you may recall, Betamax was a video recording format that competed against (and eventually lost to) the widely popular VHS format. Sony passed our Geography Test as anybody who owned a TV was a potential VCR buyer. It also passed the Feasibility Test because unlike our example of eToys.com where the technology infrastructure did not yet support the idea, Betamax in its initial form adequately solved the general public's desire to record or re-watch television and movies. The ubiquity of home VCR's in the 1980's and 1990's proves just how relevant and feasible the product was.

Not only did Betamax have a large potential customer base, but initially it also had an objectively better product in terms of picture and sound quality than its one main competitor, VHS.

Additionally, Sony had a clear first-mover advantage as well because Betamax beat VHS to the market by a year and a half.

Given this solid positioning, why did Betamax fail so soundly that it eventually became a punch line? It was because of the lack of competency exhibited by Sony management.

BETAMAX HAD A FIRST-MOVER ADVANTAGE
BUT WAS SOON OUTMANEUVERED BY VHS

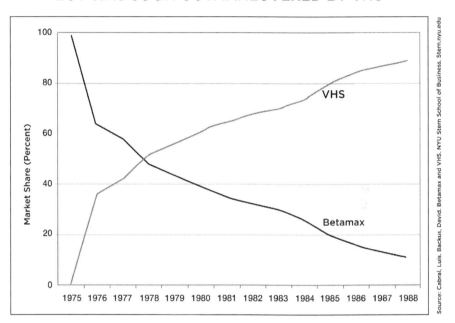

Source: Cabral, Luis, Backus, David. Betamax and VHS. NYU Stern School of Business. Stern.nyu.edu

Sony assumed they would be able to monopolize the marketplace despite JVC, one of their main competitors, pushing back and deciding not to accept Betamax as the video format standard of the future.

JVC created the comparable, but slightly technically inferior, VHS format, and then JVC management thoroughly outmaneuvered Sony.

Rather than compete on quality, JVC management made the effort to make deals with movie companies and hardware producers in order to garner a larger selection of movie titles at a lower cost.

When consumers saw that more of the movies they liked were being offered on VHS, they went with the competition, and that momentum snowballed.

Sony did not adequately assess its competency because it had nobody with the skills to survey the market landscape. Nobody in the Betamax management team had the foresight to understand the video format war would be won through strategic partnerships rather than simple hardware specifications.

So in summary, the Competency Test asks you to look at yourself and your abilities and decide if you have what it takes to bring this idea from a thought, to a company employing numerous people organized for success.

And do not forget to ask: "Am I passionate about this idea?" The greatest entrepreneurs always are, and it is what drives them to heights they themselves did not realize they were capable of reaching.

2 Identifying the Markets

Over the following pages we will discuss Identifying the Markets, some of which we already covered in the Geography Test in Chapter 1. However, through the following pages, we will go into greater depth on *why* the particular market entrepreneurs decide to commence business within is so absolutely important.

To start, let us drill down into what I mean by Identifying the Markets.

Identifying the Markets is a twofold process: First, you must decide where your traction comes from, and second, decide how scalable the overall market is. By traction, I am talking about metrics of growth that allow you to see whether your idea is actually viable in the business world. Remembering Chapter 1, metrics of growth include: profitability, gross revenue, user growth, data growth, transaction growth, deals signed, etc. At the end of the day, *some type of metric* will provide transparency into whether the idea you are pursuing is working in the market you have chosen to tackle, and often times profitability is not the initial metric that matters most.

You eventually need profitability (obviously), but as long as the firm has the resources to withstand some early negative cash flow, other metrics, such as user growth, become paramount.

Ideally, we would love for that market to be as broad as possible; however, most often in the beginning stages of business, taking time to narrow a vast market is in the best interest of entrepreneurs. Now we can look at some examples of what I am talking about.

Successful History Repeats Itself

Let us take a look at Amazon. The company first went online in 1995, after founder Jeff Bezos left a lucrative Wall Street career to try his hand in the web commerce world.

Bezos saw the e-commerce opportunity using the internet and came up with the idea of an online retail store. So basically, as we have already discussed, Bezos had an amazing idea and was in the right place at the right time.

In the 1990's technology was still a little archaic in terms of online credit card processing, but Bezos knew it was solvable through both time and money. Moreover, his idea of an online store (at the time) was fairly disruptive to an otherwise settled industry: retail.

The big companies had not yet embraced the idea of online stores, which meant an opportunity existed. Interestingly, the same thing happened almost exactly one hundred years before in the same industry.

Before we jump into how Bezos truly embraced Identifying the Markets, we should look back in history. In 1886, Richard Sears started re-selling watches to railroad station agents in his spare time from his job "as an agent of the Minneapolis and St. Louis Railway Station in Redwood Falls, Minnesota."[5]

Finding fairly quick success, Sears next hired a young watchmaker named Alvah Roebuck in 1887. Then in 1893, the two became partners and renamed the business to Sears, Roebuck and Co.

The same year, the two published a mail order catalog selling watches and jewelry. Unfortunately Roebuck left the company in 1895 due to an illness.

Sears then hired a new Vice President, Julius Rosenwald, who would become an extremely important part of the company's mail order catalog future.

---

[5] Sears, Roebuck and Co. and its Effect on Retailing in America. Martens, Beth. St. Thomas More School, Elgin. Accessed: May, 2015.
http://www.lib.niu.edu/2000/ihy000452.html

In 1896, the company published its very first general catalog which offered "guaranteed low prices, money-back guarantees, and free rural delivery, which appealed to farmers."[6]

SEARS' CATALOG IDENTIFIED THE RURAL CONSUMER BASE

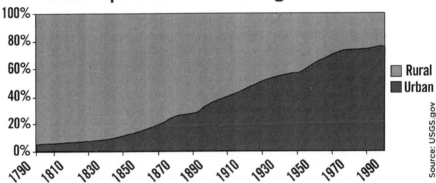

Urban Population as a Percentage of U.S. Total

---

[6] Sears, Roebuck and Co. and its Effect on Retailing in America. Martens, Beth. St. Thomas More School, Elgin. Accessed: May, 2015.
http://www.lib.niu.edu/2000/ihy000452.html

By 1908, the catalog totaled 507 pages, basically becoming the Amazon of 19th and 20th century retail shopping.[7]

So before I get down to the real message here, let us jump back to Jeff Bezos and Amazon.

Bezos knew he wanted to create the world's largest online retailer, which is why he settled on naming the company Amazon. The Amazon River is the largest and widest in the world, which was exactly what Bezos was after in terms of his retail empire. In addition, the name fit as Bezos wanted the company to be exotic and different, much like the Amazon River.

As an added benefit, when sorted in alphabetical lists, Bezos' company would show up near the top.[8] From the very beginning, Bezos understood how important branding is in today's world. After coming up with the concept and brand, Bezos needed to figure out what products to sell to the world.

---

[7] Amazon.com, Inc. Company History. Fundinghistory.com. Accessed: May, 2015. http://www.fundinguniverse.com/company-histories/amazon-com-inc-history/

[8] Byers, Ann (2006), Jeff Bezos: the founder of Amazon.com, The Rosen Publishing Group, pp. 46–47

Do you know how many products Amazon first started selling?

Here is the thing, Bezos truly understood Identifying the Markets. Defining his market(s), Bezos created a list of 20 products that could be sold online.

He then narrowed the list to: compact discs, computer hardware, computer software, videos, and books.[9]

"Bezos eventually decided that his venture would sell books over the web, due to the large worldwide market for literature, the low price that could be offered for books, and the tremendous selection of titles that were available in print."[10]

Reviewing Amazon and Sears, Roebuck and Co. there are some vital points to note in Identifying the Markets.

---

[9] Amazon.com, Inc. Company History. Fundinghistory.com. Accessed: May, 2015. http://www.fundinguniverse.com/company-histories/amazon-com-inc-history/

[10] Amazon.com, Inc. Company History. Fundinghistory.com. Accessed: May, 2015. http://www.fundinguniverse.com/company-histories/amazon-com-inc-history/

NUMBER OF LARGE BOOKSTORES BEFORE AND AFTER AMAZON TARGETED BOOKS

Leading U.S. Bookstore Chains

Spring 1991 Outlets	Fall 2011 Outlets
Barnes & Noble*: 1,343	Barnes & Noble*: 1,341
Waldenbooks: 1,268	Family Christian Stores: 283
Crown Books: 257	Books-A-Million: 232
Borders: 13	Hastings Entertainment: 146
Zondervan Bookstores: 126	Half Price Books: 113
Bookland Stores:101	Cokesbury: 57
Encore Books: 65	
Lauriat's: 48	**Total: 2,206**
Kroch's & Brentano's: 19	
Cokesbury: 40	
Tower Books: 13	
Total: 3,293	

Source: Milliot, Jim. Tracking 20 Years of Bookstore Chains. Publishersweekly.com

Foremost, it is so very important to identify the widest and deepest market possible when beginning a new company. Bezos' concept of the Amazon River is perfect in terms of what all companies want in their relative industry. Your goal as an entrepreneur is to identify the widest and deepest possible market, and then identify a product or service for that market.

Every river begins with a stream, and that is something many entrepreneurs miss. So many believe all they need is a big idea and tons of cash and their businesses will magically grow rapidly. But in the larger Identifying the Markets discussion, it is so vital to understand that every business must have a point of entry, from which it can show traction to grow into the widest and deepest river possible.

Sears, Roebuck and Co. did it through watches, and then jewelry. Amazon did it through books. But in both cases the streams led to massive rivers that led to oceans of revenue.

In both cases, the results were markets that became massive. Technology entrepreneurs often miss this point and limit themselves to small streams while endlessly struggling. Some others believe they can just dump their idea into the widest and deepest rivers of business, and then wonder why they cannot seem to get noticed, or find traction.

Entrepreneurs must "Identify the Market" twofold: First, the best market from which to prove their idea through traction. Second, the largest market their proven idea can grow within.

Sears and Bezos both identified their markets - both the streams and the rivers, and henceforth found great traction very quickly in the game.

Identifying the Market then becomes an extremely important process, and one that must be done effectively if your business is to become a success. It is amazing how many businesses fail at understanding this, and how little this very important concept is taught in business school.

Another great example of effectively identifying your market is Facebook. Facebook was founded in 2004 (as "The Facebook") and marketed to Harvard University students. Within one month, half of the university's student population signed up.

Facebook was then marketed to Boston universities, then other Ivy League schools, and eventually all US universities.

In 2005 the name was changed to Facebook.com and it was marketed to US high schools. By 2006, Yahoo and Google both expressed interest to buy the company.[11]

Zuckerberg identified the largest market possible; in this case the market was virtually everyone, everywhere.

He also Identified the Markets (streams: universities and then high schools) from which to enter the largest, deepest river.

Today, Facebook is an ocean of success and has a market value of over a quarter trillion dollars as of March 2016.

---

[11] A brief history of Facebook. Phillips, Sara. Guardian News. Accessed: May, 2015. http://www.theguardian.com/technology/2007/jul/25/media.newmedia

FACEBOOK'S EARLY USER DEMOGRAPHICS SHOW THEIR INITIAL FOCUS ON COLLEGE STUDENTS

US Facebook Users by Age Group (9/18/08) (InsideFacebook.com)

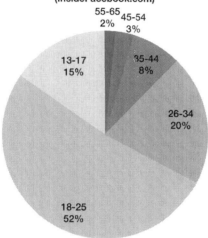

55-65 2%
45-54 3%
35-44 8%
26-34 20%
18-25 52%
13-17 15%

US Facebook Users by Age
InsideFacebook.com, 7/1/2010

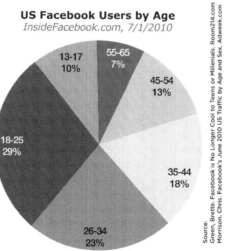

13-17 10%
55-65 7%
45-54 13%
35-44 18%
26-34 23%
18-25 29%

Source:
Green, Bretto. Facebook is No Longer Cool to Teens or Millenials. Room214.com
Morrison, Chris. Facebook's June 2010 US Traffic by Age and Sex. Adweek.com

As a side note, Zuckerberg's decision to market first to universities and then to high schools was pure genius, as college and high school students had the perfect profile of those willing to accept a new paradigm within technology, also known as early adopters.

Quickly, I want to summarize what I have just covered and then add in a few other points.

First, entrepreneurs need to identify the largest possible market their idea can succeed within.

The broader the base, the higher the ceiling. Or in Bezos' terms, the broader the base, the deeper the river.

Second, every river begins with a stream. Entrepreneurs often miss this point, and either attempt to dump their idea into the global river of commerce, or pick a meandering worthless stream that eventually dries up to deploy their concept within.

Either way, these unfortunate entrepreneurs believe in their idea, but they just cannot seem to understand why the world never took notice and why the idea failed.

Third, Identifying the Markets is a twofold concept. The first part is to allow the idea to prove itself through traction; the second is for the company to grow into a massive success.

Additionally, I would like to point out a few things. While there are exceptions to what I am talking about here, understanding the crucial importance of Identifying the Markets could very well give entrepreneurs an edge that others miss.

Moreover, much like Uber identified the first stream of business in San Francisco, and then entered the global river; Sears, Roebuck and Co. and Amazon entered the retail industry with one product and then grew to become rivers of commerce.

Facebook did the same as it grew from streams of universities and high schools into a river and an ocean of social media.

All of the aforementioned success stories were scalable on a massive, global level but began from smaller, isolated, fluid, and provable streams.

Also, and this may be a side note, but as business proves time and time again, disrupting an old industry with a new idea that utilizes technology in a way the big companies are yet to understand can be immensely profitable.

Sears, Roebuck and Co. disrupted retail through innovations in printing and railroads (both technologies) at the turn of the 20th Century.

Amazon succeeded in disrupting retail by utilizing the internet near the turn of the 21st century.

Uber disrupted the taxi industry by employing the strength of a cell phone app, and new very accurate GPS technology, something the established players had yet to employ.

At the end of the day, find the largest, deepest river you can, but enter it through a stream and disrupt it through innovation.

Apple Watch Disappointment

The Apple Watch is not going to succeed to the level the company expects; it is a duplication of something that is already perfectly fine. The product is more of a fad than a disruptive innovation.

I predict that the Apple Watch will drag on Apple's profitability for years to come; and I am stating it here. While the product may eventually find a market in the fitness and/or medical markets, the Apple Watch just is not a winner in the short-run.

To better understand why I am confident in this prediction, let us examine the Apple Watch based on the concepts I have discussed in the book to this point. In the end, I will place heavy emphasis on Identifying the Markets to build my case.

To start our conversation, let us understand what a watch is and why it matters (or not) to consumers.

Watches tell time. Things on your wrist that do not tell time are either jewelry or handcuffs.

Before cell phones, watches were important, as without a clock in near proximity, it was hard for most people to be on time to their engagements and appointments.

Over the years, the watch industry was able to grow primarily through the necessity of the function of the product first, and then through the trendiness of the fashion second.

Swatch watches were a perfect example, as were Rolexes. Swatch watches were a great example of a company disrupting a traditional industry through technology.

For those too young to remember the Swatch watch in the 1980's, here is a recap. Basically, the first modern Swatch watches were unveiled in 1983.

The watch market had become saturated with products cheaply manufactured in Asia, as seen through the rise of Seiko and Citizen.

What made the Swatch watch disruptive was that the company revolutionized the way analog watches were made, "using synthetic materials and assembly technology and reducing the number of components from 91 to 51 without compromising on accuracy or quality."[12]

In short, the watches were cheap, trendy, and appealing to the masses.

The aforesaid aside, one fact remains prominent: People still needed watches to tell time. Swatch just utilized technology to disrupt the industry, and thus created an edge.

Consequently, by the fifth year of the Swatch watch, the company produced its 50 millionth watch; by 1996, the company had produced 200 million.[13]

Again though, people still needed watches.

---

[12] The History of Swatch. Potter, Stephanie. NAWCC / Watchnews. Accessed: May, 2015. http://watchnews.nawcc.org/the-history-of-swatch.html

[13] All About Swatch: Chronology. Always-Surprising.com. Accessed: May, 2015. http://www.always-surprising.com/index.htm

But people do not need watches anymore. Everyone has a clock on their cell phone, which according to Daily Mail, people check on average more than 1,500 times a week.[14]

That is 214 times a day, or assuming most people are awake for 17 hours a day, 13 times an hour. So who uses a watch today?

The answer is anyone who likes fashion, likes jewelry, or refuses to buy a cell phone.

What I am saying is the need for watches is as dead as the *need* for payphones. Everyone has another source in their pocket.

All of this leads us to the Apple Watch. Apple has a history of disrupting industries through new technologies that innovate and challenge massive markets with products people find they just cannot live without.

But people have already figured out they can live without watches. Do you see my point?

---

[14] How often do YOU look at your phone? Dailymail.com. Accessed: May, 2015. http://www.dailymail.co.uk/sciencetech/article-2783677/How-YOU-look-phone-The-average-user-picks-device-1-500-times-day.html

So what makes the Apple Watch important? According to Apple, the Apple Watch is an extension of your iPhone, presenting users with notifications of events, a calendar, GPS navigation, and messages. In addition, and probably most importantly, the watches track your heart rate, act as a fancy pedometer, and play music. And yes, the Apple Watch tells time too.[15]

So basically, the Apple Watch is a poor man's iPhone, with a display on your wrist. The Apple Watch is priced at $349 for the base model, but most versions are over $500.

Here is where the watch might have a future: health and fitness, and that is about it. Everything else, you have your smartphone for, and given that you already check it more than 1,500 times a week, you probably do not need a watch to tell time.

On the health and fitness fronts, I can certainly see many fitness lovers wanting the product for the heart rate monitor, and other related abilities including the pedometer, which counts your steps and calculates daily burned calories.

And there are likely other health-related functions as well that will appeal to fitness buffs with a savvy sense of design.

---

[15] Watch. Apple.com. Accessed: May, 2015.
http://www.apple.com/watch/technology/

At $500 though, will consumers really jump at the product when there are cheaper solutions available already?

Looking forward, Apple sees the watches tracking blood-sugar, air pressure, altitude, temperature, ultraviolet light exposure, sleep, blood pressure, and more.[16]

On a medical front, the Apple Watch could find success; however, many other companies are already rushing to produce wearable health-related tracking devices.

A quick search on Google shows hundreds of products, and almost all are much cheaper than the Apple Watch.

The research company GlobalData predicts the mobile healthcare gadgets market to increase from $0.5 billion dollars in 2010 to $8 billion in 2018.[17]

---

[16] 9 Things to Expect from Apple's Apple Watch. Theverge.com. Accessed: May, 2015. http://www.theverge.com/2014/9/5/6108515/Apple Watch-rumors-news-apple-event-what-to-expect

[17] Mobile Technology 'Modernizes' Healthcare Sector as Gadgets Support Patients With Chronic Conditions. GlobalData, Inc. Accessed: May, 2015. http://healthcare.globaldata.com/media-center/press-

To me this prediction is much too low and clearly there is room for growth in the wearable medical products market.

But when one considers the global smartphone market was worth $266 billion in 2013, with just over 1 billion units shipped, and 1.89 billion units expected to be shipped by 2018[18], this dwarfs wearable medical products.

So is Apple trying to enter the relatively small wearable medical products market with its Apple Watch, or is it trying to create its own market? It appears to me the company is trying to create a new product category, let us call it "smart watches." I believe that people do not need these devices and are either interested in watches for jewelry (as they are not needed to show time anymore), or are looking for specialized devices that offer health data for fitness. Anyone who understands our concept of Identifying the Market is likely to be scratching their head at the Apple Watch, especially with its high price tag, when

---

releases/medical-devices/mobile-technology-modernizes-healthcare-sector-as-gadgets-support-patients-with-chronic-conditions

[18] Global Smartphone Market Analysis and Outlook: Disruption in a Changing Market. Lenovo / CCS Insight. Retrieved: May, 2014. http://www.lenovo.com/transactions/pdf/CCS-Insight-Smartphone-Market-Analysis-Full-Report-07-2014.pdf

there are so many other new and established products already competing in the marketplace as specialized watches (for jewelry) or health devices (for fitness advocates).

All of the above would - at first - point to a failing proposition in the Apple Watch for a company known to be a savvy innovator and disrupter of technology and industry.

Apple got lazy and forgot everything Steve Jobs stood for. The company is chasing trendiness. Really, it just feels like the company is trying to force a new product, and in the case of the Apple Watch, it is just not going to work.

But here is the thing, while I do believe the Apple Watch is in big trouble, there is a need for wearable fitness gadgets and medical devices.

As I already stated, I believe the above research from GlobalData is probably wrong. It is not taking into account how important wearable fitness and medical gadgets will be in the future, and I also believe the company has significantly undervalued the future market of the devices.

So what I am saying is while Apple may have some genius in developing a wearable fitness gadget with the Apple Watch, they have gone about it all wrong. No one wants the watch for the same functions and apps they can use on their phone. However, for the fitness and medical device possibilities, there certainly appears to be good opportunity. The issue is the watch is much too expensive in comparison to other products that are already leading the industry.

Take Fitbit for example. The company currently manufactures six wearable fitness gadgets ranging from $59.99 to $249.99. The most popular model retails for about $129.99, and has nearly all the capabilities of the Apple Watch, and even more so in the area of fitness tracking.

BUZZ FOR FITBIT CONSISTENTLY OUTPACES APPLE WATCH

Since September 2014, Other Wearables Have Had Higher Peak Interest than Apple

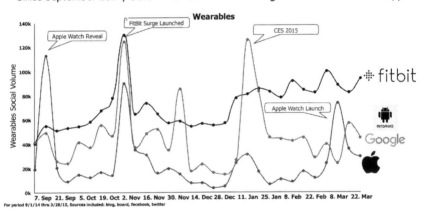

So basically, there is already a successful product available which has gained credibility and branding, and it is substantially cheaper than the Apple Watch. Moreover, Fitbit understands that to attack a market, you first must follow a stream to a river.

The company is using the fitness market as the preferred segue to establish its market. Whereas, Apple is just trying to shotgun market the Apple Watch to all areas of wearable gadgets, without specifically focusing on one particular avenue to gain market share.

It feels like Apple is banking on its die-hard customers to be willing to pay more for the Apple Watch in a market where there are already cheaper, more-established and reliable products.

So to recap all of the above in terms of the concepts within this book:

Observation of Need: Do people need watches anymore? No, their phones already tell time. Do people need heart monitors and medical gadgets? Many in the fitness group definitely want heart monitors and other health-related app capabilities. The medical needs group already has other products to choose from, however, and will continue to do so in the future, and they are much cheaper than the Apple Watch.

Most recently Under Armour has signaled it will enter this market as well. In the end, my bet would be on a device that gives customers what they truly want, without the added bells and whistles they already have on their smartphones. And I believe companies like Under Armour and Fitbit understand this better than Apple.

The Geography Test: Do people everywhere need a new watch? No. Do people everywhere need another device that already does what their smartphone does? No. Do people everywhere need or want a more expensive fitness product? Not unless they are just hardcore Apple fans most likely. Do people everywhere need a wearable medical device? Not everyone, but I feel this market will expand dramatically in the years to come. Many people with conditions like diabetes could definitely use a wearable medical device today.

The Feasibility Test: Does Apple have the management and resources to see the Apple Watch through to market? Yes. Is the technology and infrastructure in place to support the Apple Watch? For the most part, yes.

In terms of Identifying the Markets, has Apple identified a market for the product that is wide and deep like the Amazon River? Not really, because as I have already stated, Apple is really just shotgun marketing the Apple Watch to the world, marketing uses for the watch people do not really need or want: the same functionality that is easier to use with their phones.

In all aspects of the Apple Watch, it is a limited macro market because the sub-products already have competitors producing cheaper products, and they really are not focusing on the markets that could lead to the greatest profitability and traction: fitness and medical.

Has Apple identified streams that lead into a larger Amazon River of commerce - streams allowing the Apple Watch to quickly catch on? No. The fitness and medical markets are streams to larger markets and traction. At the end of the day, the Apple Watch in its current state does not disrupt any industry, and it is really just a less capable smartphone with fitness and medical possibilities on your wrist, in a world where people already have smartphones. And it costs at least $349, much more than comparable or even superior models that focus on health and fitness.

Apple Watch profits and Apple's earnings over the next few years will determine whether I am right or not. All I can say is the company should be thankful it still has such robust sales and profitability through its iPhones, iPads, and Macs. While the Apple Watch may eventually find its place, the product in its current form is going to drag on the company's bottom line for years to come, in large part because they failed to abide by the rules of Identifying the Market, which I have laid out here.

3 Building Your Company

To start this chapter let me say there are entire books dedicated to building companies. What I want to accomplish here is to give you the most important concepts about building successful firms, and I ask that you please look to other sources for additional ideas on this topic. I do believe what I include here is sufficient as an outline for successful firms, and if you follow this blueprint you will avoid many mistakes that entrepreneurs make when growing their firms.

We will first discuss building your team, which is the most important part of building your firm, and then finish the chapter by discussing other areas of concern as your firm grows.

Building Your Team

There is an old saying that states if you are the smartest person in the room, then you are in the wrong room. This could not ring any truer than in evaluating candidates to work for your company.

The first hires you make are some of the biggest decisions you will make during the life of your firm. They will shape the firm's future as greatly as you will, and so their selection is tremendously important.

Remember when we were talking about evaluating your competency back in Chapter 1? This same evaluation process must happen every time you look to grow your employee base. And here are the biggest questions to ask yourself when you look at a new prospective hire:

1. Are they technically capable in the area for which they will be responsible?
2. Are they morally sound?
3. Can they be incentivized to work at an extremely high level?
4. Will they remain loyal if given reasons to do so?
5. Are they able to work on a team?

Now let me dive deeper into each of these questions as they are all important and all of these questions will need an emphatic "Yes!" in order to make a new hire a worthwhile investment.

Remember, I say investment, because these are people you will be investing time and resources in, you may be providing benefits for these people and trusting them with classified information.

Every employee you hire must be looked at as an investment, and anyone you have to fire or who leaves to join a competitor is a failure on your part to accurately evaluate them at this stage - the time *before* you hire them. And remember, your first few hires will shape your firm possibly as much as you will, so these decisions are crucial ones. Now let's get into each question individually, listed in order of importance.

Are they technically capable in the area for which they will be responsible?

This question is an obvious one I will admit. What I want to stress here is when I analyze a prospect for her capabilities, I spend very little time on resumes. A resume is simply that first test to allow you to pare down the candidates in case you have a large number of people you are considering. There are bullet points on a resume that may be important to you, but I am suggesting that you only use resumes to weed out the least capable candidates, and when you are down to your final few candidates their resumes should be worthless at that point.

If you have 30 people applying for one position, there is nothing wrong with simple resume tests in areas such as their education, and their relevant job experience, but if you are down to say four or five candidates, it is time to throw the resume out and make the rest of the process more qualitative.

Some of the best employees I have ever hired did not go to Ivy League schools, and did not have prior experience in the exact task I wanted. What they had was the ability and *willingness* to learn what they had to in order to be successful. This does not mean you hire someone with no experience to be your CTO! What I am saying is that getting to know a person through the interview process is so much more important than evaluating their resume. When the candidates get down to a handful, throw the resumes out and look them in the face and talk with them.

The next step is to evaluate their technical competency through the interview process. In order to do so, you must know what skill set you are after. At my trading company, we were always looking for candidates who were able to analyze a lot of data quickly and accurately and then make rational decisions often using limited information. This is the basic skill set of a trader. So we developed a list of questions our interviewers could ask to help determine the candidates' abilities as a trader. The key here is knowing what you are looking for and then adapting your questioning toward finding that perfect candidate. In our case, we took many questions from IQ tests and other tests of quick quantitative analysis. But you may be looking for programmers or sales people, and therefore you must adapt your questioning for the skill set you need. I often said I met some brilliant people who made terrible traders, and that was because there are qualities needed beyond simple IQ. Ability to manage risk, emotional stability, and ability to take direction are also qualities we needed, and so those IQ questions were only used to establish if the candidate had enough quantitative analytical ability. But as I said, many smart people cannot trade their way out of a paper bag! So further questions were needed to evaluate their emotional stability and even evaluate if they can be trusted. More on the trust issue later.

So to summarize this first test: know what you want in this employee, use a resume only to eliminate candidates who are obviously not qualified, then develop a set of questions that help you quantitatively and qualitatively evaluate your best candidates for the skill set you need.

Are they morally sound?

Going down the list in order of importance leads us to the question of the candidate's morality next. How can this be the second most important question right after their technical capabilities? This can be debated, and there may be successful entrepreneurs who will put this further down the list. But I have to say in my twenty years of experience as an entrepreneur that the biggest mistakes I made in hiring were in failing to recognize I had hired someone who I just could not trust. It has cost me multiple millions.

Some people are better at reading people than others, and this soft skill is important in evaluating prospects for their moral character. Literally it comes down to looking that candidate in the eye and asking yourself, "Can I trust him?" But there are ways to help you answer that question other than relying on your gut.

Certainly thorough background checks are a must, and a few calls to his listed references also need to be done.

This should give you a good idea of his past, and if no red flags appear, you are most of the way to assessing the candidate's trustworthiness. But I would say one further step should be taken.

At some point during the interview process you should spend time with this person away from the office. I would suggest your final interview stage should be lunch or dinner and a drink out, and it should last a few hours.

Can you completely read a person in that period of time? Maybe not even the best at that skill would be able to say yes, but seeing how a person behaves when he is away from a work environment has always helped me look at the entire person better and often better assess his moral makeup.

Remember, I list a person's character highly on our checklist of questions, and this is because I have been burned by hiring people I ultimately could not trust.

You could have a brilliant candidate in front of you, but if he has flawed morals he will never use that brilliance for the betterment of the team, and it is best to just take a pass on this person.

There is a chance things would have worked out, and quite possibly this person will go on to do great things in his career, but it is not worth the chance he would cause a problem that may be so large it could cripple your young firm.

Can they be incentivized to work at an extremely high level?

This is the third question to ask yourself when hiring a new employee. I will suggest later in this chapter how important creating incentives is in driving growth in your business.

So is this candidate someone who is driven to succeed? Is he or she going to push themselves beyond what they thought were their limits if properly incentivized?

It is your job to create the proper incentives, and it is also your job to find the people who will benefit the most from those incentives.

This is another subjective area in analyzing your prospect but an important one nonetheless. Ask yourself, has this person exhibited outstanding results in his life if properly incentivized?

I love to hire people who have had success in sports, not because I want a bunch of jocks around my firm, but because they often know how to work on a team, and importantly they are often driven to succeed if proper goals are given to them.

You can use the interview process to gauge their level of competitiveness, but also remember it must be competitiveness within a set of rules, otherwise the candidate would not qualify based on the previous question of morality.

Will they remain loyal if givens reasons to do so?

A fourth question has to do with whether the candidate will be in it to win it, or if this is just another job for them. Remember I have said each employee is an investment of money but often more importantly of a large amount of time as well. You do not want to help a person develop a large valuable skill set only to see them walk a year or two later to go use it for someone else. It is up to you to properly incentivize your employees so they remain happy and loyal, and it is also up to you to pick people who will stick with your firm if you treat them well. One of the things I am most proud of about my career is the low level of turnover my companies have had. And that starts by hiring people who have exhibited an ability to see a large goal through. This is why I hire college graduates, not because of the piece of paper or even the exact school they attended. It is an example of someone taking a challenge and completing the task.

I said for the most part the resume is worthless after you have narrowed your candidates down to a few. But in this case a look at the candidate's resume can be valuable. Are there instances where he spent many years completing a task or working for a company beyond graduating college? Or does this candidate appear to jump from job to job not appearing to remain loyal to his employer? And again I would go back to looking for those who have worked on sports teams, or other team endeavors like band, debate team, or charitable work for a considerable period. At the end of the day, you need to look at this person and ask, "Will this person be with me if I am a good leader to them?" It is an important question, as you will have spent much time and money on this person, and you need to ensure you will get a sufficient return on your investment.

Are they able to work on a team?

Here is a great example of how a resume does not show you the most important characteristics of a prospective employee. You are creating a company, hopefully a large one, and companies function very similarly to sports teams. To use an analogy of a football team, you may have an outstanding quarterback (you and your fellow founders) but if he is protected by an inferior offensive line, he will likely be ineffective. Look at Tom Brady for example. He is arguably the most talented quarterback of his generation; but when he gets pressure from a pass rush his numbers are average at best. I may have digressed here a little but the point is that a company must function as a team, and everyone needs to be able to work together. If you have a talented employee, but he is incapable of working well with others, it will cause friction within the organization which often times is more impactful than any talent that person has.

A group of employees that is able to work well together creates a synergy, making the entire firm worth more than the sum of its individual parts (employees). So look for candidates who have shown past work in a team environment, whether it is sports in college or high school, or past teamwork necessary in former jobs. This is important as a team needs members who work well together.

Growth beyond building your team

As I have stated earlier, entire books are dedicated to building companies. I am touching on the most important topics in this broad category. We talked about building your team, but what are the other important topics in growing your firm? Here are some things to consider.

Run a tight ship

Today's best businesses are run with incredible efficiency. What was acceptable even ten years ago as far as expense accounts and other perks is no longer the rule. It seems as though the financial crisis spurred on these changes, and I do not believe we will ever go back to those go-go years of the 1990's and early 2000's. Companies can compete in many different ways, but at the end of the day expenses matter, and all companies would like to be the low-cost producer no matter what business they are in.

So there is a fine line to walk when deciding on how much to allot to things such as expense accounts, holiday parties, etc. That line forms at the point where good employee morale meets waste. It will be your job to determine where the line is drawn, but I will caution you that your competitors may well be willing to be more conservative than you. And if they are it may give them a competitive advantage on cost, and that is a very big hurdle to overcome.

What I suggest to you is to know how to run a tight ship, with waste squeezed out of every corner of your firm, but to also know when and how to reward your employees for a job well done. We will talk about stakeholders shortly, but as you will see, your employees are very important stakeholders and their morale is of utmost importance. You should know what is enough to keep them working in an environment that maximizes their abilities and keeps them in a place where they truly enjoy working.

Raise capital when you can, not when you have to

This is a crucial thing to remember as your firm grows. Both the debt and equity markets are fickle, especially for young firms.

It is important to understand your need for capital and to raise it when markets are the most receptive.

A great example of this is in fintech. Lending Club was in a sweet spot in the Peer to Peer (P2P) lending space in 2014. P2P lending was a relatively new concept, and the use of technology to simplify it was an extremely attractive idea. Early investors in the company saw their investments soar as the company became worth well over a billion dollars.

The company seized this opportunity and went public in an initial public offering valuing the company at $6 billion and pricing the shares at $15. On the first week of trading the shares spiked over 80% to $28, making the company worth $10 billion!

It was the first IPO in the online lending space, and the market's demand for its shares was insatiable. This was a perfect time to raise capital for Lending Club, its equity was valued dearly, and so they went public.

Fast forward to the first quarter of 2016, and the company's valuation has dropped to $3 billion, just a bit over half its IPO valuation as more online lenders have looked to raise capital and concerns about the quality of the loans these companies are making have rattled the markets.

Lending Club timed their raise well and if they were to come to the market now, they would receive a valuation of half of what they received back at the end of 2014. Now you could ask if that was fair to new investors. I would answer that by saying *caveat emptor*.

Know your stakeholders and take good care of them

And while we are on the topic of investors, there is one final subject I want to discuss before we close this chapter. The subject is defining a firm's stakeholders, and also deciding on where they fall in priority when you are managing a firm.

I believe this is an extremely important topic, and as your firm grows you will need to manage the demands of all your stakeholders in order to keep them happy. So who are the stakeholders of a firm, and which ones matter most? I would first say that by definition if a party is considered a stakeholder, their satisfaction with the firm is extremely important.

There are five main groups of stakeholders in a firm and I will list them in order of importance:

1. Customers
2. Employees
3. Investors
4. Government and Society
5. Vendors/Suppliers

As I have said, all stakeholders are important and thus keeping all satisfied with the firm's performance is crucial.

As a firm grows, the demands of each stakeholder may not remain aligned, and it will be your job to manage all of these relationships.

I ranked them here because in the end, decisions must be made, and one group may need to take precedence over another in your decision making. But you will need to keep all stakeholders satisfied in order to run a successful business.

Let us talk about each stakeholder and why they fall where they do in my hierarchy.

Why would customers and employees come before investors? Here is my opinion. If you have happy customers, and you manage to keep those customers coming back through the work of satisfied and properly incentivized employees, it will show in the valuation of your firm, and therefore your investors will be happy as well.

So first and foremost, always make sure your customers are taken care of. There is an old saying in sales that "the customer is always right." Well if you ever worked at a restaurant you know that this is hardly factual. But the point of the saying is that you should always treat your customers with the utmost respect and take their feedback very seriously. The best-run companies always know what their customers want and always give them exactly that.

Second on the list of stakeholders are employees. Remember back when we were talking about selecting employees? I used half of this chapter on growing your business just to talk about hiring the right people because it is so important.

Your employees determine how your company is viewed by the outside world and your customers. Happy employees are a must in a fast-growing firm. This is why that selection process is so important. You must pick them wisely and then make sure you incentivize your employees to help them perform at their best. Incentive programs must be geared to pay off the most when performance is exactly what benefits the firm best.

At Third Millennium Trading, the incentives were huge, as our traders were paid on a straight percentage of how much they made for the firm. This is a simple but effective incentive program. Other industries may need to tailor their incentives differently, but the best incentive programs should be tied somehow to the effect the employee has on the overall value of the firm.

A properly constructed incentive program will maximize employee morale and efficiency. And the best operators of businesses are people who know how to correctly construct these incentives.

Hire the right people and properly incentivize them. It is as simple as that.

Third on the list of stakeholders are your investors, both on the debt and equity sides. As I have said, if you take care of your customers and employees you are likely to have happy investors.

One comment I do want to make here is to make sure you never leverage your firm to an unsustainable level. In other words, be careful when using debt to raise capital.

Great firms have been brought to their knees by taking on excessive debt right before a downturn in their business cycle. Properly project worst case scenarios, and then make sure you can service the debt during those downturns. Many firms collapse due to growing too fast using leverage, when many operators only concern themselves with not growing fast enough.

Again, the best operators are those who can make proper estimations of worst case scenarios and are prepared for them.

Fourth in the list of stakeholders is government and society as a whole. I put this large group here knowing that if you are in the crosshairs of government or society as a whole, it could be game over. But usually this is a manageable thing, and therefore I rank these stakeholders low. Believe me, in running a trading group the level of compliance is often daunting, but I still believe it is manageable.

Depending on how much you interact with government, you may need a compliance officer or an entire department (if you are a big bank) dedicated to your relations to society and government.

I list this group fourth, but in some ways you should treat them as first because if this relationship sours you could have a huge mess on your hands, and it could take your entire firm down.

Lastly, there are the important stakeholders who you do business with as your suppliers. Their importance is obvious, and I will simply say although you can usually find another supplier, a good, long relationship will usually ensure you are keeping your costs as low as possible. And in today's hyper-competitive business climate, cost must be contained in order to maintain your firm's competitive position.

We have discussed many topics on growing your company in this chapter. It is a topic of which entire books are written, so there is much more that can be said about this early stage of formation. But I hope what I have shared here will help to guide you as you face the many challenges of growing your business.

4 Finding Investors

We have covered some important topics already including Getting the Idea and Identifying the Markets. Now, we will dive into one of the most difficult areas of business for many small companies: Finding Investors.

Finding investors can be extremely frustrating for many, as inherently, finding people who want to invest money in a risky startup, or fund a new idea barely showing traction is basically like trying to prove the Earth is round in the fifteenth century: a certain amount of optimistic trust and understanding is required.

Even a highly capable salesman will find pitching startups a very formidable task.

The above is exactly why I am including this section in the book, because not only can it be the most overwhelming aspect of entrepreneurship, but it can also be one of the most dangerous as well. Find the wrong investor and your company could sink in the future due to bureaucracy, hurtful guidance, investor-related pressure, potential misunderstandings and lawsuits, or in the worst case scenario, loss of control of the company you have worked so hard to build.

To start, I am going to cover what types of investors you should be looking for, what they should provide, and what you should be willing to give up.

And remember, this is from my perspective as a successful entrepreneur, and someone who has successfully invested in other ventures; the blockbuster fintech success GETCO being the most successful.

Investors You Want on Your Team

Keeping it short and sweet, you want investors who:

A. Are good, honest people.

B. Offer a deal that has fair terms and pricing.

C. Have the ability to open doors, help grow business, give you solid advice in sticky situations, and importantly, are people who actually want to (and will take the time to) help.

D. You like as people and can see yourself having a positive relationship with.

E. Are willing to tell you when things are not working and help get your company on the right road to success, and do so in an agreeable manner.

F. Are easily accessible when you need guidance.

We will talk about each of these and drill down to find some serious gems. After we talk about each concept I will then also provide information on how you can find the investors you are looking for.

Find investors who are good people

This might seem like a simple task; however, if you give it some consideration, you might find a couple deeper thoughts to examine. Foremost, does the investor have a track record of successfully investing in startups, and can she say how she actually helped the company along the way? Or does the investor have a history of investments ending up in failure or legal battles?

What is more, what does the investor's personal life look like? Do they have the ability to focus their energy on helping your firm, or is their focus on other areas not related to your business? Anything without moderation is a losing proposition, especially when there are business-related obligations at hand.

Quite often in startups, entrepreneurs go to friends and family for money, so I believe I should talk a bit about this option. In general, I have no problem with including people close to you when looking for investors, as long as the friends and family (who are not usually professional investors) understand all aspects of what they are getting into and the potential for losses. You already know these people closely, and I am not saying they are bad people, but you likely know what type of drama ensues when things do not go as planned. Are these really the type of people you will be able to inform that their investment may be headed south if that should occur? Do these people, other than having been able to provide you with *"easy to access"* money provide a positive attitude, resources, and ideas to help right the ship if things run aground?

Will difficulties within your company create family or friend drama and wreck relationships? If you answered yes to any of these questions, you already know the answer to whether you should access their capital or not.

It is important to understand that most often friends and family will likely not understand the risk of the business because they are not tenured, accredited investors. Basically, if they do not understand the risk, your business relationship could quickly become very stressed, and I hate to say it, but even possibly unmanageable. It is really important to keep friends' and family's investments to a minimum in most situations.

Basically, if you do raise money from friends and family, it should not be your main source of investment capital. If you are opening up your company for friends and family to invest, it really should be because you want them to be a part of it, not because you need the money.

Lastly, stay away from investors who upon funding your company will expect you to hire their brother, uncle, niece, and nephew. Using their investment as leverage to fulfill their own needs (employing their family) is a bully technique and not good for your company. I include this last paragraph because I have seen this happen. Keep friend and family involvement in your business to a minimum, you will thank me later!

Find a deal that does not give away too much of your company

Many young entrepreneurs are so determined to get seed money, they often do so at terms that are unfair to themselves and current shareholders. Most often this is because entrepreneurs are great *idea* people, but lacking in understanding of the theory and mechanics of how to value a business. Well, I can guarantee the VC guys on the other side of the table do understand how to value businesses, and entrepreneurs need to as well.

With the aforementioned in mind, it is really the "practical application" part of this chapter that makes our upcoming discussion so important. This is not just academic textbook hypothetical stuff, this is real world information and experience I picked up along my journey to success.

While there may be other effective models out there, I believe in Discounted Cash Flow (DCF).

In plain English, DCF is where any asset (including a company) is valued as the *present value* of the *future cash flows* it earns.

We have to remember that some assets have greater value and earning power than others. For example, does a hotel on the South Beach waterfront in Miami have more earning power than a motel in Detroit?

Of course, but what discounted Cash Flow helps us evaluate is how big the discrepancy in value would be, as long as reasonable estimates can be made for future cash flows and interest rates. And the process works not just for real estate, but for businesses as well.

While there are many great books on DCF that I would recommend, two specifically stand out. One is Security Analysis: Sixth Edition, by Benjamin Graham & David Dodd (McGraw Hill Professional, 2008). Warren Buffett actually wrote the Forward in the Sixth Edition.

The second book is The Warren Buffett Way: Investment Strategies of the World's Greatest Investor by Robert G. Hagstrom (John Wiley & Sons, 1997). Wikipedia is also a solid source on DCF.

Over the following section, I will explain the basics of DCF using a real world application from my own business career. I do still recommend you look to additional sources for more information as well.

It is important to understand the strengths of this model, as well as its limitations. We have talked about sacrificing short-term profitability for traction, but yet this model needs a profitable enterprise in order to value it accurately. Therefore, for early stage non-profitable startups, the model should not be used. I include it here to give you an understanding of how profitable young firms (and all assets for that matter) can be valued using cash flow. It is a technique used by many sophisticated investors, and it is important to understand how it works, but remember that DCF is not the only model out there, and it does not work well with companies too young to earn a profit.

If your company is not cash flow positive and will not be in the foreseeable future, or if its growth rate is extremely difficult to predict, DCF is not a good method to use to value your firm. In these cases ratios can be looked at as guides to compare to other firms which may already have publicly available valuations. At the very least these ratios can be used to compare two firms in similar industries. One ratio widely used is equity value as a multiple of revenue.

Another would be equity value per unique user. There are many others, and if there is a metric, it can be used in a ratio to attempt to value a firm. Startups that are not good candidates for using DCF are generally harder to value, but by using metrics that quantify traction you can at least compare entities with similar operations.

Discounted Cash Flow (DCF)

Simply put, the math behind DCF is basically looking at your business as a series of cash flows, which would be similar to net income, but also making adjustments to exclude non-cash items such as depreciation, and then adding back cash flow related necessary expenditures, such as research and development.

These projected future cash flows are then discounted by the business' cost of capital, which represents some risk-free rate, such as a long-term US Treasury interest rate, plus a premium that adjusts for the additional riskiness of this particular set of cash flows.

This additional risk premium is used to take into consideration that these future cash flows are not as predictable as a risk-free investment, like a US Government bond.

When I perform DCF, I rarely attempt to forecast cash flow beyond five years.

Some would even argue that it is difficult (often times nearly impossible) to predict a company's growth even two or three years out.

Regardless, for our purposes here we will use five years as our forecast range, as that is a reasonable range of predictability, without going too far out into a very unpredictable future. You can then use the same model to attempt to predict cash flow for less than five years if you like.

To complete our calculation we will assume *at least* some stable cash flow to remain at year-five levels, with NO FUTURE GROWTH.

In addition, it is important to note that when we calculate for r, the final rate we are using is the Risk-Adjusted Discount Rate (RADR), which is a combination of the 10-year US Treasury rate (also called the Risk-Free Rate), and the Added Risk Adjustment.

The Added Risk Adjustment is a subjective number. It is used to take into consideration how much riskier the cash flows are compared to cash flows of US Treasuries.

To give you an example of what I mean, see the hierarchy of products below:

LOWER RISK

US Treasury Bonds

AAA Corporate Bonds

Lower-rated Corporate Bonds, including Junk Bonds

Highly rated (low risk) US Equities (like Microsoft)

Higher-risk equities, possibly with high debt and unpredictable future cash flows.

Private companies that have at least some proven track record (Snapchat or Uber)

Fresh startups with little or no history

HIGHER RISK

For Third Millennium Trading's DCF I used five percent for the discount rate (an approximation of the 10-year Treasury rate at that time), and tacked on an additional 10% as the Added Risk Adjustment. The actual math looks like:

Total Present Value =

$$CF1/(1+r) +$$

$$CF2/(1+r)^2 +$$

$$CF3/(1+r)^3 +$$

$$CF4/(1+r)^4 +$$

$$CF5/(1+r)^5 +$$

(Zero Growth Annual Cash Flow/r) /

$$((1+r)^6)$$

CFn = Cash Flow in year n

Risk Free Rate = US Long Term Treasury rate; many use the 10-year Treasury.

Added Risk Adjustment = Generally a subjective number, based on the riskiness and predictability of the asset's future cash flows.

Risk-Adjusted Discount Rate (RADR) = US Long-Term Treasury (like the 10-year Treasury), plus an Added Risk Adjustment. For most startups, it is probably a good idea to use a higher risk premium. This number could be 10 percent, or even more.

Present Value of Zero Growth Terminal Value = Present value of all cash flows after year five.

The DCF formula is a very powerful tool in valuing assets, but because it depends on some variables like cash flow and interest rates, which are often difficult to estimate especially in young, high-growth companies, the formula can lead to large discrepancies in valuations.

Additionally, the DCF formula can be put easily into a spreadsheet, allowing us to vary the cash flows and risk rates to see how the asset value would change.

Doing so also helps us evaluate a wide range of outcomes, providing a better understanding of how your assumptions can affect the ending valuation.

Even though DCF has its limitations, a basic understanding of this formula should give you three very important takeaways as it applies to valuing startups. I like to call these the **Three Rules of DCF**.

1. The higher the growth of your company, the higher your company will be valued.

2. Counter to #1, the more volatile and risky your cash flows (also the more difficult it is to calculate these cash flows) the greater the requirement for a higher discount rate. A higher discount rate will result in a lower valuation of your company.

3. If you add a VC, other strategic partner, or employee that directly increases your company's growth rate and cash flows, that person or entity could be worth a lot of money as they can significantly increase the value of your firm.

Now, I will present an example of the real world application of DCF, based on an actual experience that helped determine the success of my trading firm.

Third Millennium Trading

I started my first company, Third Millennium Trading, in 1996. The firm was a proprietary equity and options trading and market making firm at the Chicago Board Options Exchange (CBOE).

I had started with just $250,000 and grew my firm to a book value of $1 million in two years.

Even though the book value had grown, I was experiencing some financial difficulty in 1998. Basically, I needed more cash in the bank to trade, meet margin requirements, and expand operations.

Again though, my firm was basically worth about $1 million at accounting book value.

I was seeking some additional capital and found a potential investor who was willing to put in $1 million. However, he wanted 50 percent of my company in return.

Though my book value was only $1 million, I felt like I had *significant* growth potential, and giving up 50 percent of my company for book value was just too steep. It just did not make sense because I knew what I had and how much potential I had to grow.

This investor brought nothing but money to the table. In a case like mine, because I did not have to value any additional skills the investor brought, other than cash, the DCF model was very straight forward.

Here is how it worked:

First take a moment to recall the DCF formula:

Total Present Value =

$$CF1/ (1+r) +$$

$$CF2/ (1+r) \,^2 +$$

$$CF3/ (1+r) \,^3 +$$

$$CF4/ (1+r) \,^4 +$$

$$CF5/ (1+r) \,^5 +$$

(Zero Growth Annual Cash Flow/r) /

$$((1+r)^6)$$

I believed my company's future cash flows would be: $500,000, $750,000, $1,000,000, $1,500,000, $2,000,000 and because I was in a relatively risky industry, I would use a Risk-Adjusted Discount Rate (RADR) of 15%.

This would make the formula look like:

Total Present Value =

$$500,000/ (1+0.15) +$$

$$750,000/ (1+0.15) ^2 +$$

$$1,000,000/ (1+0.15) ^3 +$$

$$1,500,000/ (1+0.15) ^4 +$$

$$2,000,000/ (1+0.15) ^5 +$$

$$(2,000,000/0.15) /$$

$$((1+0.15)^6)$$

I believed all the above assumptions were conservative in valuing my firm.

Also the Present Value of Zero Growth Terminal Value was estimated as $(2,000,000/.15)/ ((1.15^6))$.

Using the above variables, the value of my firm could be seen as:

434,783 +

567,108 +

657,516 +

857,630 +

994,353 =

3,511,390 = Present Value of Years 1-5 Cash Flows

$5,764,368 = Present Value of Zero Growth
Terminal Value

$9,275,758 = Total Present Value

In short, I believed the value of my firm was much higher than book value.

Just looking at the first five years of Present Value Cash Flows, the number was much higher than book value, let alone adding in Present Value of Zero Growth Terminal Value.

Obviously there were a lot of assumptions in this calculation, but it shows that selling 50 percent of my company for $1 million would most likely have been a *very poor business decision*.

At the point when I needed the additional capital, I had just taken a large loss, so the extra equity would have really helped.

I just could not justify it though, because I really believed the company had tremendous growth potential, and the additional investment of just $1 million - *with no other added benefits* - was not worth giving up 50 percent of my company.

One thing to remember is the more an investor brings to the table - besides money - the more you should be willing to give up.

The problem in my case was, other than money, the investor was not really bringing anything to the table.

It just appeared that we were too far away in terms of what seemed agreeable. If he had requested 10 or maybe 15 percent of the company, I would have considered the deal much closer to fair and possibly would have accepted it.

Losing 50 percent was just too much in my mind, especially since I felt once future growth was factored in my company had a much higher value.

"I just could not justify it though, because I really believed the company had tremendous growth potential, and the additional investment of just $1 million, with *no other added benefits*, was not worth giving up 50 percent of my company."

Basically, when an investor's expectations of the amount of equity they should receive, based on what they are adding (in reality) are too high, it is a red flag that the investor might be difficult to work with in the future.

Why give up so much for so little?

Yes, the investor might be trying to protect themselves based on their assumption of risk, but when the investor is trying to capitalize on a downswing in the startup, or is just gluttonous from the start, it is probably just a huge red flag.

"When in doubt, stay out" is an old trading mantra that comes to mind in this particular case.

As a result, I did not accept the investment and did not give up 50 percent of my firm. And after growing my firm to over $100 million in book value within 10 years, I was very happy that I turned the guy down.

With the above in mind, we need to revisit #3 in the previously mentioned Three Rules of DCF.

Just to refresh your memory, the Three Rules of DCF are:

1. The higher the growth of your company, the more your company will be valued.

2. Counter to #1, the more volatile and risky your cash flows (also the more difficult it is to calculate these cash flows) the greater the requirement for a higher discount rate. A higher discount rate will result in a lower, but probably more accurate valuation of your company.

3. A very important takeaway is that if you add a VC, other strategic partner, or employee that directly increases your company's growth rate and cash flows, that person or entity could be worth a lot of money as they can significantly increase the value of your firm.

Finally, I do want to discuss the model's shortcomings. As we said earlier, the model is only used for companies with positive net cash flow, so many early stage startups would not qualify for this model.

Also, companies in the process of turnarounds, where cash flow can be negative would not be good candidates for this model. But for the majority of companies and asset classes, I rely on DCF as a tool to use to help estimate value.

Remember, it is simply a tool, and remember the model's limitations. Having said this, I believe it is the best tool in finance for valuing assets, and should be considered even for startups, assuming they have positive net cash flows.

Find investors who can open doors, have a special skill, can help grow business, or give you solid advice in sticky situations. And importantly, people who actually want to (and will take the time to) help, without being controlling or hindering.

As a rule, if you would not want the investor on your board, you probably do not want the investor at all.

Now, let me present an example where the DCF formula can be used to evaluate a strategic partner and may cause you to accept deals that may initially look unfair if you do not consider how this investor will affect future cash flows.

"As a rule, if you would not want the investor on your board, you probably do not want the investor at all."

Let us assume a well-known VC with large connections and wisdom in your industry is interested in investing in your firm.

For simplicity's sake you expect your firm to grow at 20 percent per year for the next five years, but with this new investor your growth rate would increase to 30 percent.

The VC bids $2 million for 20 percent of your firm. Again for simplicity, your current cash flow is $1 million. Calculating DCF with a five year growth rate of 20 percent and a 10 percent discount rate generates a value of about $20.6 million without the investor involved.

So basically, his bid of $2 million for 20 percent of your firm seems too low as it assumes a valuation of $10 million.

This is called a "post-money valuation," because I am including the $2 million in the valuation, as it is part of the $10 million firm that will exist after the investment is made.

It appears he is buying a $20 million firm for half price, why would you do this deal?

Well here is why: if this strategic VC increases your growth rate from 20 percent to 30 percent, which is certainly possible in some cases, the investment dramatically changes the value of your firm.

Without his investment, remember you would own 100 percent of a firm worth $20.6 million.

But using DCF at a growth rate of 30 percent yields a value of the higher growth supercharged firm of $29.5 million.

You also would add the $2 million investment in this and the firm's value with the strategic investor would be $31.5 million.

Now would you rather own 100 percent of a firm worth $20.6 million, or 80% of a firm worth $31.5 million (valued at $25.2 million)?

Here is an example of how a strategic investor can add enough value to make a deal that looks a bit unfair at first glance, in reality a deal worth accepting.

In the real world you may be faced with multiple suitors and difficult estimations of growth rates, but you should use DCF as a tool in helping to analyze your options. Just keep in mind it is an estimate of the value of an asset, and an estimate only as good as the assumptions you use for the variables in the formula.

Many young entrepreneurs are so eager to get seed money in the door that they make unwise business decisions, do not be one of them. Play smart, become wealthy.

When GETCO was looking for seed capital, I requested 20 percent of the company, non-dilutable for the first two years.

GETCO had several investors they could have chosen from, but because I was not trying to be greedy, and because I could help guide the founders during the fintech High Frequency Trading (HFT) startup's early years and help them make some critical decisions early on, they decided to take my bid.

The bottom line is you really want an investor who not only is bringing money to the table, but also will help open some doors, give advice or guidance, and basically help the business grow. If you have a money-only investor though, even if you really need the cash, it is never a good idea to give up too much of the company. There are times to take those bids, but make sure to properly value a value-added investor before making your decision.

Find investors that you like as people and can see yourself having a positive relationship with

Personality is a major issue, if there are personality clashes between founders and investors there are going to be major problems later on, I can almost guarantee it.

You want someone who is easy to get along with, understands what you are trying to do, and is willing to step in and help when needed, but will not try and control your company.

There is definitely a fine line between helpful guidance and unbalanced assertiveness from an investor or outsider.

This is an intangible quality, but it is important to consider nonetheless. Taking on investors is basically a marriage, and you do not want the relationship to end poorly. Just as in a divorce, it can cost you dearly.

Ask yourself, can I see myself working closely with the person for many years?

I touch on this point because although it is subjective, it can be just as important as objective formulas like DCF. A bad relationship with a key investor can wreck your business.

Find investors who are willing to tell you when things are not working and will help get your company on the right road to success, and do so in an agreeable manner

When things start to get bumpy (and in most startups, they eventually do), if you have an investor who is more worried about his money than the future of the company, the employees, or your vision as a founder, you could be in for even more stress and headaches than you initially planned for.

When things are getting off-track, you want someone who is willing to work with you in a positive manner to help get things headed in the right direction again, not someone who will use their position to leverage their input or opinions. Those who are really interested in more than just a return, but instead actually seeing your company grow and prosper are really the kind of people you would want on your Board of Directors, or Board of Advisors. They are the people you turn to when you need confidence, confidentiality, and another opinion, because you have encountered a situation that may have several outcomes you did not initially anticipate.

These business-savvy individuals are those who are intelligent, but not arrogant, and who bring real experience to the table. You want someone who is willing to listen as much as they are willing to offer advice.

Finally, we have our last point:

Find investors who are easily accessible when you need guidance

We live in a globally connected world today with all our technology. If your investor, mentor, advisor, or board member is just too busy to take your call, or meet for coffee when you really need some advice, it is probably a good idea to pass on their seed capital for someone who is more accessible. Enough said on that one.

I cannot stress enough how important everything I have just covered is. Many times young startups are willing to take almost any money just to get the ball rolling, or survive. But taking the wrong money, taking cash from someone who wants too much of your company, does not really bring anything else to the table, is difficult to get along with, or basically just is not accessible, can destroy your business, even if you have a brilliant idea. Remember there is always another investor out there; you just need to be proactive in finding her.

Keep looking until you find the right situation. Sometimes, you just have to trust your instincts, if it does not feel right, it probably is a sign you do not have the right investor.

5 Entrepreneurialism in the Modern Age

If you have done well in the other stages of business, at some point you should start seeing signs of success. I am not talking necessarily about profit, but perhaps the signs that you are on the right track might show up in other forms of traction.

As I have already mentioned, traction can come in the forms of users, subscribers, deals, traffic, or any kind of metric showing your idea is catching on.

At some point you should have a large pool of customers to sell to. In today's increasingly competitive world it is becoming more tactical to sacrifice short-term profits for increased sales.

The idea is more sales should generally equate to more customers, which really means traction. Today's startups that are not beholden to the market's demands for quarterly earnings are sacrificing short-term profits for increased sales to boost public awareness of their product or service.

Entrepreneurialism in the modern age requires that all aspects of business continually focus on acquiring customers/users, while remaining competitive to retain and grow revenue.

Small companies who are not cognizant of their respective competitors are in big trouble in today's challenging business climate.

And thus, to create an edge over your competition in the initial stages of business, it might be a good idea to sacrifice short-term profits for traction, growth, and sales.

The aforementioned is why many tech firms do not become cash flow positive for many years.

Once again, Amazon is a great example.

Amazon has never been a company focused mainly on profit. But the company does care passionately about revenue. Revenue growth and product development seem to be two of the only things Amazon truly cares about (with little profit), obviously along with creating a great experience for customers as well. However, the company continues to plow cash flow back into new business development quarter after quarter, year after year.

The company always seems to end up with little or no profit, as seen in the company's Price to Earnings (PE) ratio. When we look at Amazon's current PE ratio we see a significantly elevated projected Forward PE of 166 for the year ending December 31, 2016.[19] The projected 2016 number is much better than the staggeringly high 2012 12-month trailing PE, which was 550.[20]

Basically, one has to wonder why investors in their right mind would buy shares of Amazon if the earnings are so low with respect to revenue.

Amazon uses precisely the strategy I am talking about here. Sacrifice short-term profits (or in Amazon's case, long-term profits too) for revenue, user growth, and business development in order to position yourself better versus your competition in the future. In other words, build the moat we had talked about earlier instead of concerning yourself with short-term profitability. If you execute well, creating that competitive advantage, the profitability will come.

---

[19] Key Statistics, Finance.yahoo.com. Accessed: June, 2015.
http://finance.yahoo.com/q/ks?s=AMZN+Key+Statistics

[20] Amazon: Nearly 20 Years In Business And It Still Doesn't Make Money, But Investors Don't Seem To Care. Clark, Meagan & Young, Angelo. Ibitimes.com. Accessed: June 2015.
http://www.ibtimes.com/amazon-nearly-20-years-business-it-still-doesnt-make-money-investors-dont-seem-care-1513368

The market understands that Amazon is on track to become an annual trillion-dollar revenue company. And eventually Amazon will start dialing in profit, but for the time being, the company's focus is on revenue and business growth. The market values Amazon on a *what-if* basis, rather than on profitability.

Ultimately, Amazon is a low cost, high value-added business. And the company has a significantly large war chest of services to compete in business.

Warren Buffett likes to say, build a moat...

The concept of an economic moat can be traced back to legendary investor Warren Buffett, whose annual Berkshire shareholder letters over the years contain many references to him looking to invest in businesses with "economic castles protected by unbreachable 'moats.'"[21]

Ultimately, you want to create a monopoly without admitting you have, like Microsoft.

If you cannot get a monopoly, aim for an oligopoly like Google, Facebook, and Uber.

---

[21] What is an economic moat, and how does one determine whether a company's moat is wide? Lopez, Jeremy. Morningstar.com. Accessed: June 2015.

An oligopoly is, "A state of limited competition, in which a market is shared by a small number of producers or sellers."

I know terms like monopoly and oligopoly are not exactly the most politically correct in today's ultra-sensitive, be compassionate to the little guy world. But what we are talking about here is business. You are competing for revenue and profit, and the bottom line is if you do not compete fiercely, someone else will - and your business will be out of business.

This does not suggest that you engage in any type of dirty ethics or unscrupulous business actions. But you do have to compete, and if your business really starts to gain traction, you must build a moat to stay competitive.

One way to build a moat is to have the best technology. Another way is to have a cost advantage. Often times these two go hand-in-hand in that your technological advantage gives you a cost advantage.

Having the best technology is hard for competitors to overcome, which is where the value is in the moat.

But beware: *no technology lasts forever.* If someone does breach your moat, you are in trouble.

As an example of the moat being breached, think back to America Online and BlackBerry as examples.

America Online, which is currently owned by Verizon, provided online access in the late 1980's and 1990's, providing the internet to millions using dial-up technology. "By 2000, AOL was the nation's biggest internet provider and worth $125 billion. The company merged with Time Warner (then the parent company of TIME), and executives of the combined firm announced that they expected AOL Time Warner to grow 33% in the next year."[22]

The problem was Time Warner officials had not factored in the upcoming broadband revolution, or at least did not believe it would happen right away.

Unfortunately, phone and cable companies were already in a fierce race to provide high-speed internet to at-home users. As at-home broadband ensued, America Online, with its lethargic and bulky platform, was phased out.

America Online's moat had been breached by at-home broadband, and by 2003 the company's stock price had lost nearly $200 billion in shareholder wealth.

---

[22] A Brief Guide to the Tumultuous 30-Year History of AOL. Rothman, Lily. Time Magazine. May 22, 2015. Accessed: July, 2015. http://time.com/3857628/aol-1985-history/

AOL DID NOT ANTICIPATE QUICK BROADBAND PENETRATION

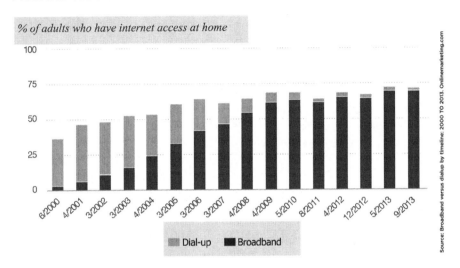

% of adults who have internet access at home

Source: Broadband versus dialup by timeline: 2000 TO 2013. Onlinemarketing.com

America Online is still alive today, as the company owns the Huffington Post along with other internet properties. But as history shows, when the moat is breached a massive reduction in the shareholders' wealth will ensue.

And how about BlackBerry, the darling professional phone that took the world by storm in the first 10 years of the new millennium? BlackBerry, if you recall was innovative in that the phone had a keyboard which allowed users to easily send and receive email and texts.

The "scroll ball" was an innovation that allowed users to quickly move through email and messages.

The BlackBerry was truly the first smartphone that allowed professionals and executives to increase productivity by being able to easily communicate while away from the office. Other phones had the ability to email and message, but none with the ease and professionalism the BlackBerry encompassed. The BlackBerry also had internet, a camera, and video starting in the later model, Pearl.

BLACKBERRY'S MARKET SHARE CRASHED AFTER THEIR MOAT WAS BREACHED

US Market Share

In 2009, BlackBerry had nearly 50% market share in U.S. operating systems, according to IDC.

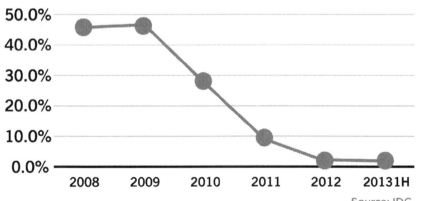

Source: IDC

Source: Benoit, David. BlackBerry's Slump in 4 Charts. Blogs.wsj.com

Basically, if you were a professional it was a given that you owned a BlackBerry. The BlackBerry was more than just a phone, it was a symbol of being an "on the go" successful business person.

The marketing of the phone was pure genius, as it was at one time believed to be a must-have device for young urban professionals.

So what happened to BlackBerry's amazing success? When you really break it down, the company became too focused on marketing and not focused enough on maintaining the moat through research, development, engineering, and innovation. That R&D became its Achilles heel was somewhat ironic, considering its parent company was Research In Motion.

Case in point, in the 2013 Bloomberg Business article titled The Rise and Fall of BlackBerry: An Oral History[23], we see excerpts from insiders explaining the situation:

> **"Lysyk:** *There was so much management. You'd have your team lead, then your manager, director, then senior director, then another*

---

[23] The Rise and Fall of BlackBerry: An Oral History. Bloomberg Business. Felix Gillette, Diane Brady, and Carolin. December 05, 2013. Accessed: July 2015. http://www.bloomberg.com/bw/articles/2013-12-05/the-rise-and-fall-of-blackberry-an-oral-history#p4

director. At one point they said it was [only] 5 to 10 percent engineering. That's pretty hard for a tech organization.

Washington: *Lazaridis used to come into these meetings, and it was almost like Pulp Fiction, where he'd open the case and there would be this golden glow of devices. We were all super eager to see it. Around 2007 the glow was getting a lot smaller every time he came around."*

Tyler Lessard, the vice president for global alliances and developer relations, stated BlackBerry just did not see new technology or other types of phones as a threat. In the same Bloomberg Business article he states:

Lessard: *You saw these iterative products coming to the market from Microsoft and Palm. There were so many devices where people said, "Oh, this one will take on BlackBerry." There was a sense of confidence in the company where we thought, "It is not going to happen." The same thing definitely happened when Apple introduced the iPhone.*

The bottom line here is really that a strong product overtaking the bulk of market share can sometimes lead to a sense of overconfidence and refusal to see how and where up-and-coming competing technologies could be about to breach your moat.

And I think this is an interesting point to make very clear. I call it the Success Arrogance Destruction (SAD) Syndrome. If at any moment you find your company in an elevated stage of success, it is very important to do a reality check to make sure the SAD Syndrome has not set in: And that it is not hindering you or your innovators from seeing threats attempting to, or getting ready to attempt to, breach your moat.

As they say, "Necessity is the mother of all inventions." And when someone else is hungrier than you, it is very possible you are going to need to work twice as hard to keep your competitive edge, especially in the world of technology.

I call it the Success Arrogance Destruction (SAD) Syndrome. If at any moment you find your company in an elevated stage of success, it is very important to do a reality check to make sure the SAD Syndrome has not set in: And that it is not hindering you or your innovators from seeing threats attempting to, or getting ready to attempt to, breach your moat.

In the end, having the best technology is your edge, and if because of arrogance, bureaucracy, or just plain laziness you have stopped innovating your technology, you have opened the door for a competitor to breach your moat. <u>I cannot stress this point enough.</u>

Politics Matter

Finally, I want to share a few quick thoughts about politics and charitable giving from your start up.

Most important, be willing to play the *political game*, because if you are not doing so your competitors surely will be.

You will have to make sure to stay on good terms with government and especially regulators. In some cases you should even bring in people from the regulatory side, and be sure to stay in the good graces of any organization that might have weight in your industry.

Regarding charitable contributions, it is nice to give back to the community, but remember you are in business to maximize long-term profitability. There are organizations that are given special tax status to help communities, they are called nonprofits. Unless you are a nonprofit, do not forget you are in business for a reason: to create growth, turn a profit, and increase the wealth of your shareholders. Remember the hierarchy of stakeholders discussed in Chapter 3: your customers, employees and investors should always come first.

But we also have to remember that some level of giving back allows for greater community public relations and a more amicable business environment, which also can mean higher profits.

No matter what though, we remember that while giving charitably (from the company) is always tempting, most often when doing so you are hurting long-term profitability, and you are doing a disservice to your long-term stakeholders, employees, and others.

My advice is, unless giving serves value to the company and shareholders, keep charitable contributions to an individual level.

The primary goal of the company should be profit maximization. Rising tides lift all boats, as in, when the company is doing well it can employ more people, make more money for shareholders, and create substantial wealth, allowing for greater individual giving to the community.

Do not forget it, and also do not forget to play the political and networking game.

6 Exit Strategy

In the world of venture capital, "exit is everything," which is why Chapter 6 is so very important to all entrepreneurs.

I am assuming readers are seeking to eventually exit their companies, or are seeking some type of partnership, buyout, merger, or other structured deal, to at the very least, partially cash in on their hard work.

Over the following pages, I will cover four ways to exit your company: sell to a competitor (full exit), go public (partial exit), sell to private equity (partial or full), and continue to stay private (partial exit).

Each of these has its own merits, and as we will see, each can be the correct choice of exit.

Sale to a Competitor

Sale to a competitor only happens when you make your company so valuable to a competitor that they would rather buy you than compete with you.

In essence, you have created or obtained a technology or segment of the market cheaper to buy than to create, obtain, or compete with.

You have created or obtained a moat of great value that is not easily breached. Whether it is through a technology, user group, or market segment, you have created an asset of value.

Building an asset of value that is attractive to a competitor is not easy to achieve, but if you can - and do - your company can be sold much quicker, at a higher multiple than in the open market.

What I mean by selling quicker than in the open market is you have something so valuable that instead of advertising your willingness to sell to the whole world, there are already firms who will immediately jump at the opportunity to purchase your asset of value.

Case in point, in February of 2014, Facebook paid $22 billion for the chat platform startup WhatsApp.

What is amazing about the sale is "WhatsApp's total losses were close to $138 million in 2013 alone, against revenue of $10.2 million."[24]

WhatsApp agreed to sell to Facebook for $19 billion (which increased to $22 billion after Facebook's stock appreciated), when it was valued privately at a tenth the price. WhatsApp had unique users that Facebook thought would be easier to buy than to compete for.

This is a great example of a company being valued by competitors much higher than the overall market valued it.

Why would Facebook pay so dearly for WhatsApp, when the company was valued at only 10% of that price?

----

[24] Facebook's $19 billion acquisition, WhatsApp, lost $138 million last year. Dhapola, Shruti. Tech2.com. Oct 30, 2014. Accessed: August 2015. http://tech.firstpost.com/news-analysis/facebooks-19-billion-acquisition-whatsapp-lost-138-million-last-year-239338.html

THE POSITION OF WHATSAPP AS THE MARKET LEADER IN MANY MARKETS MADE IT VALUABLE TO FACEBOOK

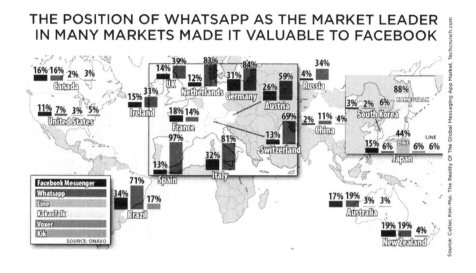

Source: Cutler, Kim-Mai. The Reality Of The Global Messaging App Market. Techcrunch.com

WhatsApp had what Facebook wanted (unique users it needed to grow its business more quickly), and Facebook decided it was easier to pay for these users than to try to acquire them on its own.

Many analysts and pundits questioned this deal when it was originally announced, but they are certainly not questioning Facebook's performance since the deal.

Obviously Zuckerberg knows what he is doing, the question is, do you know how to create something that a firm like Facebook has to have?

Going Public

Going public is a very long process. Your company has to meet the standards of one of the public exchanges, the NASDAQ, the NYSE, or another public exchange in a foreign market like the LSE in London, the Dax in Germany, or the Hang Seng in Hong Kong. They have minimums for sales and market capitalization although your firm does not have to be turning a profit.

This is why it takes a while to qualify. Firms usually need at least five years to get to the size required to go public.

Going public is definitely a viable exit strategy, but it is a long and arduous process.

There is also a large amount of public information your firm will be required to provide once you are a "listed stock," including the filing of quarterly 10Q reports that inform the public of your overall financial health including earnings and current balance sheet numbers.

Because the filing requirements and overall red tape involved in becoming a public company are so demanding, many firms stay private. You do not have to educate the public of your fortunes which often times provide information for your competitors. But if you are able to go public, you then have a liquid market for your firm's equity and thus you now know what the firm is worth without having to sell the entire company, or even lose control of it. And you also have a source for more capital, in case you need to raise money in the future.

There are ways to structure the firm with multiple classes of stock that allow you to sell over 50 percent of the equity but not lose voting control of the company. These multiple-tier stock companies allow for each tier to have different voting rights.

A great example of this structure is Alphabet which, many readers are likely aware, was formerly known as Google. This was done to better separate Google's core businesses from its more ambitious and riskier ventures. Investors will more easily be able to see the performance of these two very different business segments as separate entities when Alphabet reports their earnings.

Alphabet has three classes of common stock, two with voting rights, and one that has no voting rights. Founders Sergey Brin and Larry Page announced in 2015 they would reduce their equity holdings in the company. After the proposed sales, Brin and Page will own 11.9% of the company's voting class A and class B shares, yet they will still hold 52% of the voting power. This is possible because of Alphabet's structuring of their various classes of common stock. Class B shares, mostly owned by Brin, Page, and Chairman Eric Schmidt, hold 10 times the voting power of the Class A shares. These Class B shares are often referred to as "super voting" shares. The Class C shares have no voting power at all. By owning the vast majority of the super voting Class B shares, the founders have been able to maintain voting control even as they divest some of their interest in the company.

Private Equity

A third exit strategy is a partial or full sale to a private equity group or other similar third party. A sale to private equity involves the agreement to sell all or part of the company to a private equity group, but a sale could be to any entity. You can sell your entire firm or just a portion of it. This event often allows some minority shareholders to "cash out," and allows the founders to at least get a portion of their capital out of the company.

Because you are selling directly to another entity and the public is not involved, the filing requirements are much lower. The onus is on the buyer (caveat emptor), and thus large requirements of the seller will be needed during the due diligence period prior to the sale.

The main reason to choose this option is obvious; the sale of the entire firm at once relieves the owners of significant financial risk. The buyer often requires the founders to remain on for a period of years to help with the transition and also in some cases continue to lead the firm. But this is a way to take some, if not all of your chips off the table.

Another reason to choose this option is if the buyer is a strategic partner, and the sale is only a partial sale; which will create a synergy with the buyer often due to increased scale. Also the buyer can have expertise or technology that will improve the business. Because there are no required minimums for sales or other metrics, this option can happen earlier in a firm's life and because the valuations can still be quite high, this is often an attractive option.

GETCO chose this option and was partially acquired by private equity firm General Atlantic in 2007, which is when I sold most of my equity in GETCO. As a seller, you have to be cognizant that the buyer in this case is a very educated buyer, and therefore very price sensitive.

Private equity firms like General Atlantic are highly intelligent groups, and if you are selling to them you have to understand there is a risk that you are selling too low. But in the case of General Atlantic's purchase, I felt very confident that the time was right.

GETCO had come a very long way, and although the future looked extremely bright, it was hard to imagine that competitive pressures would not increase in the near future.

My partners and I sold GETCO at a valuation of $1.7 billion in 2007, and the firm's valuation based on its portion of the public firm KCG Holdings is less than half that amount as of the end of the first quarter of 2016, almost nine years after our sale.

Remain Private

The last option is one that really did not exist ten years ago. At least the amount of liquidity in the private markets for firms was nowhere near what it is today. Today, firms like Uber remain private and raise millions and sometimes billions of dollars privately from large investors and funds.

Hedge funds have begun to participate in these private funding rounds, and recently even mutual funds have been open to this risk.

Ten years ago the thought of Fidelity looking at a company like Uber was unheard of, as the risks associated with that type of investment were viewed as prohibitive.

As I said earlier, public companies are required to file a large amount of information so that the public, including large mutual funds, can be confident in understanding the public firm's business and financial performance. But in private funding rounds there are much less onerous information requirements.

Once again, the onus is on the buyers to do their due diligence when a transaction is proposed. This precluded bigger players from these deals and significantly reduced the liquidity. But in this era of low yields, many firms, especially hedge funds, have decided to venture out into the riskier investments and have been willing to look at these private deals.

This is great news for entrepreneurs who never would have been able to remain private in decades past. There are now hundreds of private companies with valuations of over a billion dollars, or as they call them in the VC world - unicorns. This is a very recent development and it means that remaining private indefinitely, and thus, not needing to meet the filing and size requirements of a public company, is a viable option in the current market environment.

The one negative of this route is a big one though. Even though there is a viable market for funding these private companies, it is nowhere near as liquid as the public equity markets, and thus, most firms choose to go public when they get to be large enough to do so.

Examples of firms who have remained private even at a size where going public is possible are Uber, Lyft, Airbnb, and Snapchat, among many others. As I said, there are presently many unicorns out there, which are billion dollar private firms, versus ten years ago when there were virtually none. And the option to remain private has never been more viable than it is today.

7 Summary

Starting a company is without a doubt one of the most challenging things you can do in your life. If successfully done it can also be one of life's most rewarding accomplishments as well. What I have tried to do in this book is cover the entire adventure from getting your idea and how to know it is an actionable one, all the way until you are looking for a partial or full exit from the business. Let us look back at the key takeaways.

Every great company was started with an idea, a way in which to improve the world. The people who are best at coming up with these ideas are the best observers, or "super observers," who have the ability to figure out what others need often before these other people even know they need it.

A great idea takes into account where the world is heading, not just where it is now. A famous quote from Wayne Gretzky said that great hockey players know how to skate to where the puck is going to be, and that same concept works for ideas. Always look to skate to where the puck will be, do not just react to where it is now. And do not forget to take advantage of how technology is changing and how that will affect your idea.

Another attribute of a great idea is that it can work on a global basis, or at least appeal to a large group of people, and is scalable. This we called the Geography Test, and it is important when evaluating your idea.

Later in the chapter we talked about the Feasibility Test. Can your idea show traction? Are there metrics that show your idea is taking hold? And does technology exist to allow for the idea to succeed? Many of the dotcom busts of the late 90's were simply too early. The technology and infrastructure necessary for them to succeed was not in place yet.

Lastly we mentioned the Competency Test, the ultimate question being: "Are you the right person for the task?" And also are you passionate about this project? The key here is if you can answer these questions honestly and accurately.

The greatest entrepreneurs always are passionate about their ideas, and it is what drives them to heights they themselves did not realize they were capable of reaching. So are you up to the task? Do you have what it takes, and will you be able to face the long odds of starting your own business?

Once you have determined the quality of your idea and if you have the ability and desire to bring it to market, you must identify that market. This process was discussed in Chapter 2. Ideally we want as deep a market as possible, one that allows your idea to gain traction.

Entrepreneurs often begin small, with one product, possibly in one city. But the best ideas are highly scalable, allowing for the company to grow quickly into multiple products and/or across a large geographic area. The moral here is: identify a large market, start at a pace based on your current capital and workforce, but then allow your company to scale as quickly as possible before your competitors do. This is only possible if your idea has identified a sufficiently large target market. If it has, and you manage your growth well, your company should be highly successful.

We completed the chapter talking about why I believe the Apple Watch in its current form will be a disappointment due to its lack of identifying a large market.

The Apple Watch does not bring anything new to the watch market, but simply duplicates products that are already in existence and does not better them. Time will tell if I am right.

In our third chapter we discussed how to grow your company. There are entire books written on this topic so I focused on the major issues, and to me the most important one is hiring employees.

These people, especially your early hires, may contribute as much or more to the success of your company than you will! And remember, if you are the smartest person in your company, you probably have not done a great job hiring people.

There are five main questions you need to ask yourself when hiring people and they are in order of importance:

1. Are they technically capable in the area for which they will be responsible?

2. Are they morally sound?

3. Can they be incentivized to work at an extremely high level?

4. Will they remain loyal if given reasons to do so?

5. Are they able to work on a team?

If you can answer these all in the affirmative, you have yourself a good hire. Grab that person and make sure you pay and incentivize him well.

Next we talked about running a tight ship, meaning keeping your operations as efficient as possible. We mentioned the fine line between spending to keep your employees happy, and wasteful expenditures. Knowing what costs are necessary for things such as expense accounts and holiday parties is an important part of keeping your firm efficient.

We also talked about the importance of raising money when your company's equity and debt are in high demand, rather than waiting for when you desperately need the capital. Smart companies raise money when they can, not when they have to.

We finished Chapter 3 by identifying your company's stakeholders, and prioritized them in the following list:

1. Customers
2. Employees
3. Investors
4. Government and Society
5. Vendors/Suppliers

It is very important to keep all stakeholders happy, even though at times their needs could be conflicting. It is a challenge to run a growing business, but it can be done, it has been done by many others, and if you follow my guidelines, you can succeed in doing so as well.

In Chapter 4 we discussed raising capital. We identified the type of investors you want: good, honest people at a fair price. You want people who can open doors for your company and help it grow.

It is also important the investors are people you can work with amicably, but are also willing to tell you when things are not working and help you to change things for the better. Lastly, you want investors who are accessible in case you need their guidance.

We discussed a model for valuing assets called Discounted Cash Flow (DCF), pointing out that although it is the best model for valuing assets, it is not always applicable to young startups if they have no near-future projections of positive cash flow, and/or their growth rates are too difficult to estimate.

If DCF cannot be used, ratios such as Price/Sales and Price Per Unique User can be used to value a business. These are not ideal but in the case of startups, no model is ideal for valuation.

We also talked about how adding a strategic partner could significantly increase the value of your business and how that may make adding them as an investor much more attractive than bringing in silent partners who will do nothing beyond funding your growth. I gave you an example of the math behind this concept, and showed there can be a dramatic change in your company's valuation when you bring in the right strategic partner, one which adds significantly to your earnings growth.

In Chapter 5, we talked about some strategic decisions you should make as your company gets larger. It is often a good idea to focus on gaining traction in the form of the number of users and total revenue rather than focusing on short-term profitability. Amazon comes to mind when talking about using this strategy brilliantly.

We talked about Warren Buffett's saying about building a *moat*, which is an advantage that gives you a leg up on your competition that is not easily circumvented.

Ultimately the ideal is to create a monopoly, like Microsoft enjoyed in the 90's and early twenty-first century. And if you cannot get a monopoly, strive for an oligopoly like Google, Facebook, or Uber.

We talked about ways to create your moat, and that technology is the most obvious and often the best way, but that if your advantage is breached, you are going to have large problems regaining this advantage. If it happens without warning it could even spell disaster for your firm.

The final parts of the chapter discussed the Success Arrogance Destruction (SAD) Syndrome and how to avoid it. And also we discussed the importance of playing the political game. Whether you like it or not, this may be something you are forced to do in order to protect your company and its stakeholders.

And finally our Sixth Chapter discussed exit strategies for your firm. There are many ways to partially or fully exit your company. You can sell to a competitor (full exit), go public (partial exit), sell in a private sale (partial or full exit), or sell part of your firm in the private markets (partial exit).

Each of these methods has its own merits, and your choice depends on what is available to you and your goal for your exit.

A sale to a competitor is a clean break and can offer a very high price as long as you have created an entity your competitor can not easily create on its own.

Going public is a very long, tedious process, but the result will be a liquid market for your company's stock. Once public, your company will have very arduous reporting requirements and its performance and operations become an open book for the entire world to see. But in return, you will get constant feedback from the marketplace on how your company is performing, and usually it will be relatively easy to raise further capital if needed.

A private sale, often times to a private equity group, requires much less as far as filing requirements, and there are no minimums as far as revenue or market capitalization like there are with public equity offerings. This is a good option when you are looking to sell the entire firm, or if your firm is too small to go public.

A final option, which did not exist ten years ago, is to remain private and continue to sell some of your equity without using a public exchange. Because large investors like mutual funds and hedge funds are now looking to make investments in startups, it is now possible to sell large parts of your firm without ever going public, even if you are big enough to do so. Companies like Uber have chosen this route and continue to fund themselves in private markets and may never go public due to the amount of liquidity available that did not exist in the past. Firms who choose this route do not have to meet the strict filing requirements of exchanges, but still are able to sell significant parts of multi-billion dollar enterprises. The drawback to this approach is that this market is still not as liquid as the public equity markets.

I hope the book provided you a great deal of useful information as you decide whether the entrepreneur's life is for you. As you can tell, starting, running, and eventually possibly exiting a company is a tremendous challenge. But I believe it also can be one of the most rewarding experiences of your life. If you do decide to go down this path, I wish you good luck and hope this book helps guide you in a successful endeavor.

Epilogue: Letter From Michael J Palumbo

Here are some thoughts going forward about technology and its effects on current and future macroeconomic conditions:

We are in some interesting times. Stock markets and commodity prices have fluctuated wildly over the past decade, and recently we have seen interest rates and commodity prices move to extremely low levels compared with what was forecasted just a few years ago. How many forecasters saw oil dropping from over $100 a barrel to under $40 this past year? Or thought interest rates on long-term government bonds in developed countries would remain near zero? Some of these bonds actually are currently trading with a negative yield (like German bunds for example), which means you literally have to pay the issuer of the bonds for the right to hold them.

I would like to close this book with my thoughts on how technology and entrepreneurs have affected some of these macro trends and my predictions on how many of them will play out.

Let us first focus on inflation. Throughout history, the biggest drivers of price inflation in commodities or anything of value have been the relentless increase of human population driving demand and the fluctuations of supply.

High inflation has always been accompanied by either some shock in the supply of a commodity like what happened in the 1970's in crude oil, or just an increase in demand usually driven simply by more people, especially as these people enter the middle class.

Oil prices last decade soared as anticipation of a large number of people, especially in Asia, entering the middle class reached a fever pitch, and calls for "peak oil" rang out in the markets as fears rose that supply was dwindling.

What happened next was simply technology and entrepreneurs reacting to an opportunity. The US reacted by introducing modern fracking techniques which dramatically increased the supply of oil, and for the first time in modern history, the nation was relatively self-sufficient in its oil needs. But why did oil plummet over 60% in less than a year?

In deflationary moves, always look to technology first. Not only had the US and other nations found a way to dramatically increase the output of oil, entrepreneurs invested in alternative energy sources which took away a large amount of future oil demand. These sources include solar, wind and nuclear energy.

But still you may say much of this has been coming for a while now, and people should have known enough to gradually reduce the price of oil. Also China, the world's largest importer of many commodities including oil began to show signs of a slowdown.

The final straw was as oil began to slide, OPEC nations which produce a large percentage of the world's oil, and Saudi Arabia in particular, started to signal to the market that they would not cut oil production to prop up its price. When this became apparent the bottom dropped out of the market, and we now have oil trading at a level not seen since the beginning of the century.

The question you have to ask yourself is will this continue? In the past, any significant drop in oil prices was temporary and oil rebounded to new highs only a few short years later. But I believe this time it is different.

No doubt demand from emerging economies like China can drive overall demand higher, and population growth is expected to rise worldwide from just over 7 billion people to 10 billion by 2050. But the trend toward alternative fuels is not going away, and population levels are predicted to remain steady beyond 2050.

I believe that oil producers see the writing on the wall and that is why the Saudis have refused to slow production. Why stop selling at $40 a barrel when in a few years it may be lower still? I believe the era of "peak oil" is over, and you can thank technology and entrepreneurs for this.

Always remember that inflation is generally driven by population increases, and deflation is often times caused by technology. So you entrepreneurs out there can be proud to know your fellow men and women may have ended the high prices of oil once and for all.

Let us talk about another area of technology and how it is affecting our global macroeconomics. This area is in job creation and reduction due to artificial intelligence.

Throughout history entrepreneurs have caused dramatic changes in technology, which have caused many people's skills to become obsolete almost overnight.

There are many examples of this throughout history such as assembly workers, parking lot attendants, and more recently floor brokers. Remember my example of GETCO and how that company and its technology in high frequency trading caused many to lose their jobs in the trading industry as computers took over the role traditionally played by brokers and even some traders.

In the past, for every job that was lost due to technological change, another was gained of higher value (higher pay). So even though times of technological change had caused severe pain as the workers' skills were required to be modified, in the long run, employment was bolstered by a whole new group of higher value-added jobs.

But what is happening in the current economy? For the first time in history, innovation in artificial intelligence seems to be making human tasks obsolete at a faster rate than it is creating new tasks.

This trend has only been happening for a few years now but the results are causing a drag on employment numbers, more so in the quality of jobs offered as opposed to the quantity of those jobs. Unemployment rates in the U.S. have returned close to levels before the great financial crisis of 2008, but the quality (and pay) of these jobs has not been as high as is typical in an economic recovery.

The number of those left unskilled and unemployed seems to be remaining high, and in many countries where skilled labor in technology is low, these numbers are going higher.

We may be facing a situation here where this time it is different. This time technology and entrepreneurs may be causing unemployment and underemployment to rise, and this trend may continue for the foreseeable future.

What if promises of driverless cars come to be true soon and result in job losses in trucking, which currently is an industry with huge employment?

What are these people going to do for work?

We could be heading for some very serious issues as governments are forced to confront how technology and entrepreneurs are causing so many to lose their jobs.

Nations will need to retrain workers in technology and soon. And nations will also have to deal with the possible increase in the amount of people who want to work but cannot find a job.

Maybe it is my conservative leanings, but I have never been an advocate for large safety nets for nations, mainly because in the past many of the people using these safety nets were gaming the system and had no desire to work. But if trends continue in technology, governments are going to have to have serious discussions on increasing these safety nets for the millions of displaced workers and also help them to learn new technologies.

What you should take from this is simple: You either have to have the skills to tell a computer what to do, and for that you will be paid very highly, or you will be in a job where the computers tell you what to do, and those jobs will not pay so well. This is a concept I tell young people all the time.

Lastly, I would like to discuss how technology and entrepreneurs could be affecting the currency markets and how this may play out in the future.

As we have seen in 2015, the dollar has been on a big run and the dollar index rose to its highest level since early last decade. The currency has remained relatively strong through the first quarter of 2016. I believe technology has contributed to this rise.

The US economy has weathered the conditions that have followed the great financial collapse of 2008 - 2009 better than all other major economies, and I believe America's strength in technology is a huge contributing factor.

America is still the center of entrepreneurialism as it has been for over one hundred years. And the current business climate puts a premium on technology. As I have stated earlier, technology has affected the commodities markets, and it has also caused the balance of geopolitical power to tilt towards countries that lead the world in new ideas.

This is always the case, but today it is more so than any time in at least the last one hundred years, and you may have to go back to the beginning stages of the Industrial Revolution to find a similar time.

My feeling is that the dollar has further room to run based on the country's comparative advantages in technology.

The time we live in no longer puts a premium on commodities that you dig out of the ground.

Thanks to technology, much of these natural resources, in particular dirty sources of energy like oil and coal, are slowly being phased out.

Countries that are leaders in technology are going to be well positioned for the coming global economy.

Countries that depend on commodities will continue to struggle for the foreseeable future. This is why you see countries like Russia and Brazil in depressions, while the United States is able to continue to grow albeit slowly.

I expect this to continue as the world adjusts to what technology is forcing upon it. These changes are necessary and welcome as they will reduce the cost of energy to the world and also allow it to produce this energy much more cleanly. But in the short term it is causing a lot of pain in commodity-based economies.

So expect the dollar to continue a good run as commodity countries remain very depressed. They will need to adapt to this new normal and develop new comparative advantages in order to recover.

This definitely has destabilized the world and has caused a lot of hardship. But as I have said, it is necessary for the world to adjust to the new normal of technological change.

Adapt or die, and Brazil and Russia are finding this old adage out the hard way.

Nations that lead the world in technology will have a comparative advantage that is hard to beat and the United States appears well positioned for this new world.

Again, I hope you have enjoyed my book. The world is changing quickly. These changes are both exciting and terrifying. But those skilled with the right tools and driven to work hard should find no better time than now to succeed.

Calculated Risk: The Modern Entrepreneur's Handbook

About Michael J Palumbo

Michael John Palumbo (born October 28, 1966 in Chicago, Illinois) is an American business magnate, ex-CBOE (Chicago Board Options Exchange) floor trader, entrepreneur, venture capitalist, and sports enthusiast.

Palumbo is the founder and controlling partner of Third Millennium Trading, LLP., Third Millennium Trading, LLC., and TMT Investments, LLC., all Chicago-based proprietary trading and market making firms.

Palumbo is also the principal of MJP Capital, LLC., a private Midwest regional holding company focusing on both real estate and technology. The two main ventures of MJP Capital are Ceres Acquisitions, and CeresTech.

Palumbo is known for turning $250,000 into over $100 million within 10 years of founding Third Millennium Trading, LLP. (TMT) in 1996.

Palumbo is also recognized as the original venture capitalist who provided the initial funding for the high frequency trading firm GETCO.

In August 2007, VH1 featured Palumbo in the documentary The Fabulous Life of Wall Street Billionaires – Ballers. Also in 2007, Palumbo was highlighted in the book Trade with Passion and Purpose.

Index

Made in the USA
Lexington, KY
30 December 2016